# MEMOIR OF AN UNIMAGINED CAREER

43 Years Inside
Mennonite Media

Melodie M. Davis

***Memoir of an Unimagined Career:***
***43 Years Inside Mennonite Media***
by Melodie M. Davis



Printed in the United States of America
Cover and Interior Design by Elizabeth Petersheim



Library of Congress Control Number: 2022939200
International Standard Book Number: 978-1-60126-800-6

Masthof Press
219 Mill Road | Morgantown, PA 19543-9516
www.Masthof.com

Dedicated to my husband, Stuart, and millions (billions?) like him who worked long hours and years in hardscrabble factories and warehouses—through summer's sweat and winter's chattering teeth. The world would not function without all the men and women like him.

"Girl in a chicken house longing to be a Christian writer produces national TV documentaries for Mennonite churches." This could be an alternate subtitle for Melodie Miller Davis' four-decade career at Mennonite Media. Her memoir is a must-read for those who relish the power of women in media, the gifts of mentoring, and joy in one's calling. Memoir fans, church history buffs, and lovers of authentic stories will enjoy this book!

-Marian Longenecker Beaman, author of *Mennonite Daughter: The Story of a Plain Girl*

Melodie Davis adeptly tells the history of Mennonite Media and the endless projects that emerged. Her story will resonate with all who struggle to find meaning in their work and how to navigate a room full of ideas. The range of media and topics she worked with is impressive. Her insights about collaboration, admitting failures, pushing the edges, caring deeply about the people in the stories and embracing changing opportunities are nuggets of wisdom to glean. She doesn't overlook the institutional frustrations or the foibles of her colleagues but deals with them graciously just as she did in person over those many years.

-Jerry Holsopple, PhD, Professor of Visual & Communication Arts, Eastern Mennonite University

"To be a writer:" finding words to convey the wonder of new visions and heartening stories as she lives and works through 40+ productive years, this is the story Melodie Davis tells in a memoir of her working years.

-Margaret Foth, author and speaker on the national *Your Time* radio program produced by Mennonite Media for ten years

Anyone who has memories of the *Mennonite Hour* as it grew into what is now MennoMedia will love this book. Melodie's personal story woven into this church agency's story makes this a fascinating read!

-Harvey Yoder, semi-retired licensed counselor at Family Life Resource Center and pastor of Family of Hope Mennonite House Church

# Table of Contents

# Acronyms Used in This Book

ABC – American Broadcasting Company

CBS – Columbia Broadcasting System

CCM – Council on Church and Media

CRTC – Canadian Radio and Television Commission

CMU – Canadian Mennonite University

DJ – Disc jockey

EMC/EMU – Eastern Mennonite College/University

GPS – Global Positioning System

IMMG – Inter Mennonite Media Group

JELAM - Junta Ejecutiva Latino-americana de Audiciones Menonitas, a Spanish board for broadcasting ministries in Latin America

MB – Mennonite Brethren

MBC – Mennonite Brethren Communications

MBI – Mennonite Broadcasts, Inc.

MBM – Mennonite Board of Missions (later named Mennonite Mission Network)

MCC – Mennonite Central Committee

MCUSA – Mennonite Church USA (name after 2001 merger of Mennonite Church and General Conference Mennonite Church)

MMN – Mennonite Mission Network

MPN – Mennonite Publishing Network (earlier named Mennonite Publishing House)

MYF – Mennonite Youth Fellowship

NBC – National Broadcasting Company

NCC – National Council of Churches

NCCCC – National Council of Churches Communications Commission

NRB – National Religious Broadcasters

NPR – National Public Radio

PSA – Public Service Announcement

TAT – Television Awareness Training

WLR Foods – Wampler Longacre Foods

# Foreword

It was an exciting time to be part of Mennonite Media—we had multiple radio programs, national TV public service spots, our first series of video storytelling, auxiliary print resources including books and newspaper columns, a recording studio, a mass market book distribution ministry and more.

We worked with media internationally, collaborated with other Christian groups across the country and worked hand in hand with our Canadian counterparts. This little organization in the Shenandoah Valley I first knew as Mennonite Broadcasts touched people's lives all over the nation and in other parts of the world. We were known nationally for the creativity and quality of our work. These Mennonites were definitely not "the quiet in the land!"

During my more than a dozen years with Mennonite Media in the 80s and early 90s, it is not even a stretch to say that Melodie Davis was the hub of all of this activity. She managed speakers, wrote scripts, wrote promotional copy, and edited much of what the rest of us did! As a young producer, it would not have crossed my mind to proceed on a project without consulting with her.

Fast forward 25 more years and Melodie is still authoring books, managing a web presence and writing a regular newspaper column that appeared in various newspapers across the country. I was proud to open my local paper and see her byline there, her writing always crisp and interesting and written in a way that represented the Mennonite/Anabaptist understanding of the Gospel so well.

In this book, *Memoir of An Unimagined Career*, Melodie reminds me that, as she says, Mennonite Media had "a mindset favoring innovation in the organizational DNA." Her later chapters describe TV network documentaries, video curriculum, a ministry website and much more that grew into a ministry I could not have even imagined. And there were still later years when Melodie returned to a more traditional publishing role of managing editor for the new parent publishing company, MennoMedia and Herald Press.

In Chapter 15, Melodie reflects on her 43 years of work: "I felt…a connection to the even wider circle of God's family that we had sought to reach through the multiple forms of media that we embraced at Mennonite Media. Sometimes a little wobbly or fumbling, but always seeking to bring praise and insight to the God of our lives."

I'm grateful for Melodie's commitment to our church community and ministry and witness for 43 years with Mennonite Broadcasts, Inc., through several name changes and parent agencies to the MennoMedia of today. Many things have changed during these many years, but Melodie's constant and consistent creativity, insightfulness and steadiness, all in helping others follow Jesus, did not. I am grateful that God has blessed her ministry through these many years and that I had the privilege of working with her for a season.

*Ron Byler is the former executive director of Mennonite Central Committee U.S. and the former associate executive director of Mennonite Church USA. He served in several roles including executive producer of Mennonite Media Ministries from 1979-1993.*

# Introduction

This book is for anyone exploring careers or jobs or a path for their lives—whether you are 18 or 81—and wanting to find God's direction amid your own aspirations. (If you smirk about "81," remember Grandma Moses was 71 when she began her art career.) It is also for those enjoying reflection on their own work life and past experiences.

As you might guess, it would be impossible to include all of the highlights and activities and productions of a church-wide agency covering the years I worked at Mennonite Media (with its various names) from 1975 to 2019. The goal of this book is to share memorable stories of the far-flung media outreach of this small but creative and committed staff, bloopers and all. We'll dig inside to reveal the workings of this agency as it endeavored to communicate the love and compassion of Christ on issues of the day to an increasingly secular public. Along the way, you'll be reminded of the amazing advancements in technology during these 40-some years.

Whether you are a memoir fan, an historian or church history lover, wanting to pursue or pivot to a job or career in media or communications, wanting to find out more about Mennonites, or just love quirky but true stories, I hope you enjoy this book. I hope you'll indulge me the personal tidbits and stories I share along the way and let them trigger your own memories, thoughts, and goals. You can be or do more than you even imagine.

And now, to the chicken house!

CHAPTER 1

# It All Began in a Chicken House

My writing career began accidentally when six incarcerated men shuffled into the gymnasium at Middlebury School (Middlebury, Indiana) in handcuffs for a scare-them-straight assembly. I was in seventh grade in 1964 and I think the assembly included sixth grade through seniors.

Armed guards stood on either side of the mock jail cells represented by steel bars, set up like a makeshift cow pen. The men stood behind the bars and one by one told the story of how he landed in Michigan State Prison.

I felt nervous and excited about what could happen in the presence of these bad guys. Most of my classmates were listening intently, almost spellbound. You could hear every cough and sh-sh-shush from a teacher in that mostly still gymnasium. Would they try to escape in that low security setting? What would the guards do?

My teacher asked us to write an essay on the experience afterwards and she submitted mine (and perhaps others) to the local *Middlebury Independent* in the event the paper might want to publish one or more.

When my essay was published, I had my first taste of byline glory: By Melodie Miller. What a rush.

I don't know when I started enjoying writing things down or making up poems, but it probably came about because I liked being praised by my teachers (doesn't everyone?).

Many of us have had teachers or guidance counselors or youth group sponsors who have encouraged and helped mold the direction of our lives—perhaps unknowingly. On the other hand, a guidance counselor of mine in high school was sure I was "college material" and counseled me in that direction, but at the time I was pushing back against the status quo and he made me a little rebellious on the topic of going to college.

Why go to college if you didn't know what you wanted to be? Why spend (or borrow) all that money? Some of my friends would be getting married soon after high school (this was 1970) and starting families, which sounded sweet and homey, but new voices were pulling many of us in new directions. How do you find the right path anyway? Some get directed into a non-college path and spend too many years regretting that decision.

After seeing my essay published, the young ego was content for oh, maybe one week. Seeing my name, words and thoughts in the paper was a big happy dance for the brain. I needed more. But how would a seventh grader ever get so lucky again?

Perhaps my sense of self needed stroking because I was the third child in a string of four, with my brother—the beloved son—being born last. I adored him, but I was just a third daughter. "Oh, another girl" I can imagine my father sighing when he saw the evidence. Unlike other dads at that time, he was allowed in the delivery room because the doctor was tardy. Once the doctor got there, I'm told they discussed the ins and out of raising chickens, a theme we'll pick up in this book later. Dad coveted a boy, of course, to help him on the farm in those gender-stereotyped 1950s.

To be fair, we were all well-loved and well-treated, if you didn't count the birthday spankings. One of my siblings hated the annual smack down so much that on one birthday—once she got wise to the ritual—came downstairs for breakfast with a hardback Nancy Drew book inside her pajama pants. She had tucked it between her underwear and skin, nicely shielding her rear end. When Dad swatted, it sort of pained his hand. That didn't make Dad happy at all, I seem to recall.

I was praised by my parents for being "so good." Several days after I was born, my mom lay hemorrhaging in her bed at home. My dad was out working at the time. She was frightened, because she knew she needed help. She felt she could die from bleeding out if she had to get up and tend to my needs. She had heard of prolonged hemorrhaging killing young mothers. She always said I just lay sleeping peacefully in the bassinette and didn't cry. No texting her husband to get the heck home. She became undyingly grateful for my agreeable disposition.

Mom also treasured the name she had found for me in a book written by one of the very few Mennonite writers/novelists at the time, Christmas Carol Kauffman. A sweet character's name was "Melodie Ann." I think I tucked Mom's admiration for this novelist's prolific and engaging writing in the back of my head.

Which, in a long roundabout way, led eventually to memorable times in our chicken houses.

Gathering eggs twice a day and even on Sunday was our job from when we girls were strong enough to carry the yellow wire egg baskets "collecting" eggs (as my citified cousins called it) in our early chicken houses. But gathering eggs (the real term) was a chore we didn't mind because it provided us children with a regular income. Twenty-five cents a basket wasn't "chicken feed" for a seven- or eight-year-old child in 1959. Later, we went "modern" with a 10,000-hen cage layer house (no more loose chickens, unfortunately for the hens) and earned even more. The hens spent their lives in cages suspended from the (then huge) chicken house, with the putrid chicken manure piled a foot or so high underneath the cages. There were sidewalks between each row of cages. The inventors, of course, paraded the "more sanitary" conditions for chickens and eggs.

On those sidewalks we pushed carts normally holding 1,440 eggs—gathering them twice a day. For this chore we were paid a penny a flat of thirty eggs, often earning fifty cents to a dollar a day, and five to ten dollars a week, depending on how many times we worked. Dad also hired a neighbor woman, Lorene, to help my mother gather eggs in the forenoons[1] when we were in school.

Sometimes one of my siblings, who shall remain nameless, enjoyed throwing eggs into the manure especially in the summer when it was all runny and rank from the heat, sloshing the legs of whomever was in the next aisle. Eventually she tried that on friends brought home from school for overnight. I don't remember ever doing that to my friends but of course I laughed when she did it, so which is worse? But never mind that; she was fun-loving and very popular, a fact that did not go unnoticed by me as a much shyer younger sister.

I spent most of my time while in the chicken house daydreaming about what I would grow up to be, reflecting on my Mennonite faith (which only permitted Sunday work like gathering eggs and feeding animals, no field work), and boys. I also sang to the chickens, and enjoyed watching them cock their heads sideways at me, likely in horror at my sometimes off-tune voice. If I went opera on them or gobbled like a turkey, which I loved doing, they responded with a swelling chorus, cackling back.

It was in this earthy, smelly place of great contemplation and musical excellence where I first penned out my ambition in life on a scrap of paper. I still have it to this day, hidden in a file.

> "On this day, November 18, 1967, Saturday afternoon at 4:30 p.m., I decided what I want to be: a Christian writer."

I was 16 years old and by then had my first poem published in *WITH* magazine, our church paper for teens—my second snort of the addictive drug called "Byline."

---

1 "Forenoon," now a mostly archaic reference to mid-morning roughly from 9-12. But common lingo in my home.

In retrospect I felt just a bit of holy awe as I wrote those words down, with no idea—not a clue—of how to get there as a young farm girl. Everyone else and my two older sisters were aiming for more traditional careers for women of the day: nurse and teacher.

What would people say if I said I wanted to be a writer? I had been a faithful reader of the Mennonite church Sunday school papers and publications over the years put out by the denomination's publishing house in Scottdale, Pennsylvania: *Words of Cheer, Youth's Christian Companion, Gospel Herald, Christian Living.*

But a writer doesn't just write for bylines in church publications and ten-dollar checks. Writers want to make sense of things and perhaps offer a hint or a help to others going through dilemmas. Some people need spread sheets, equations, formulas. Writers need sentences and paragraphs.

• • • • •

I was born in 1951 in Sarasota, Florida, where my parents sojourned six months that winter, along with other northern Mennonites and Amish testing out farming options in the warmer South.

At about the same time, the organization where I would work over 40 years—Mennonite Broadcasts and later Mennonite Media—was also being birthed up in Virginia. My future boss, Ken Weaver, began working there when I was barely four.

In the spring of 1952, we moved back to northern Indiana where my name was dutifully entered on the cradle roll of North Goshen Mennonite Church. A cradle Mennonite, I went to Mennonite camps, served in a Mennonite Voluntary Service program one year, and finally ended up at Eastern Mennonite College (EMC) in Harrisonburg, Virginia—not wanting to follow my sisters to much-closer Goshen College.

My path as a writer can also be directly traced to my piano teacher and pastor's wife at North Goshen, Martha Krabill. She patiently sat as I stumbled through three or four years of Schaum piano books. For that alone she deserves a Grammy. Perhaps she knew I'd never make it as a musician. So, it was a blessing that an idea of hers, shared with her son, James, led to my very first regular column in print.

James Krabill was editor of our high school paper at Bethany Christian High School, *The Reflector*. Years later, he would be the departmental director of the larger organization I worked for. As editor, James was searching for a columnist to profile selected members of the senior class through the year. As I remember it, he wanted someone to interview seniors and write a short, interesting sketch of what made them tick—and what they hoped to do in life.

Martha suggested that James ask me, on the basis of short features I wrote for our church newsletter at North Goshen about youth group activities. I always tried desperately to be more creative than just a straight up report like "The MYF (Mennonite Youth Fellowship) enjoyed the hayride and Halloween party at the Miller barn the other week..." (How boring.) James was also in a creative writing class with me my sophomore year. Miss Hoover, our teacher, frequently read our writings aloud to the class. Those were always occasions for red cheeks and squirming inside: to have private thoughts shared out loud while secretly enjoying the fact she had picked something from your writing.

Ideas for future career paths are sometimes sparked by field trips or youth group experiences. When the "Sunshine Girls Club" from my church toured the *Chicago Tribune,* that certainly got my blood pumping. I've always loved the smell of diesel in a city coming up from subways. Or, in Chicago, the L-train. I was thrilled seeing the workings of a big city daily newspaper. Inside the office of the *Tribune*, the desks were piled high with papers, clackety typewriters, and smartly-dressed women in high heels (this was the early 60s). People dashed around breathlessly like they had important deadlines. Would I ever be able to work in a place like that?

I craned my head to see if there were any young "copy boys" or girls in the mix. I had read a youth-reader type book, *Copy Girl,* which I loved. Wikipedia says the job is now archaic and describes it as once a "common position at many papers for a younger worker."

So I never was a copy girl but I began earning my writing creds in the years after high school. At EMC (now Eastern Mennonite University), there were not yet any communication studies or majors. But one of my high school/church friends, Chuck Kauffman, recommended me to one of the editors at the college newspaper, *The Weather Vane.*

A first college newspaper writing assignment writing about what students had done over the summer, thrilled my bones. I felt I was already headed to a beat with the *Chicago Tribune*. But the feature editor, Gretchen Hostetler, was aghast at my work. She said it sounded too "high school-y." She soon reined in my immature flairs and she became a fun-loving mentor.

I took a work-study job my senior year of college at WVPT-TV, the public broadcasting station in Harrisonburg. On one of my first days there, I had to run a studio camera when they were short a camera person, taping a local public affairs show. I was rudely introduced to the longest string of profanities my young Mennonite ears had ever heard when one of us failed to move the camera at the right time. The *&^%$ was piped directly into my ear from the director. But that TV work-study job on my résumé impressed my future employer—at least that is what I heard from my boss later on. The *Weather Vane* writing experiences in college also yielded many samples I could use in a portfolio.

By the time I graduated from EMU I had, along with every other graduating senior, a bad case of senioritis—the disease that affects you toward the end of your senior year of college when you just want to be done. Seniors also want to be able to tell people what they're going to do next. I sent out a bevy of query letters, résumé, and writing samples to Mennonite agencies who might need a budding writer. I also sent queries for writing jobs in areas where I had family, or in communities where I thought I'd maybe want to live. Nothing. Polite robonotes came back saying "We'll keep your résumé on file."

My Spanish professor was one of those asking me what I was going to do after graduating. He was maybe not my most favored professor but he was quite adequate and seemed to express a genuine interest in my studies and future after I took his Spanish lit class. "I'm looking for anything that has to do with writing," I said.

He knew my major and first love was writing. I was an English major, even though I'd ended up with a minor in "modern languages" after my junior year of study in Spain and taking a semester of German.

"You might want to try where my wife works," Sam offered. We irreverently called most of our professors by their first name at EMU. My ears perked up. His wife, I knew, was Ella May Miller, the speaker on a popular Mennonite radio program of the time, *Heart to Heart*. My friends who worked at the college radio station used to croon the program's "Love at Home" theme song, an old hymn we knew from our childhood.

"Oh?" I said, or something equally non-committal.

"One of the secretaries is leaving," he explained further. My heart rather fell. Secretary?

But then he offered a somewhat limp endorsement, perhaps sensing my non-excitement. "You have much more communication background than many of their hires."

I thought, well, if I got a job there, I could stay in Harrisonburg where my boyfriend lived. For now.

So it was that I started work at Mennonite Broadcasts, Inc. (MBI), about one month after graduation in 1975. I never thought I would work there beyond five years at most. Didn't most people usually change jobs about every five years?

AS FAR AS EYE CAN SEE — This chicken coop at the Vernon U. Miller farm, six miles northeast of Goshen, extends as long as a football field. Constructed of redwood rather than the usual aluminum chicken house, the building is ventilated in the summer with fans.

HOW TO GATHER AN EGG — Mrs. Miller gathers eggs not in a basket, but into a "flat" which is placed in the egg crates. Mrs. Miller can easily push approximately 100 dozen eggs on the steel carts where the flats are placed.

*Melodie's mother, Bertha Stauffer Miller, gathering eggs in the 10,000-hen chicken house (huge at the time), circa 1966.*

*The Mennonite Media building circa 2010; several restaurants rented part of first floor for a few years each.*

CHAPTER 2

# The Waning Days of *Heart to Heart* Souvenir Spoons and the Fifteen-Minute *Mennonite "Hour"*

In the year that I was born, *The Mennonite Hour* preaching and music radio program, which I would grow up to work for, first went on the air in Virginia. The year was 1951. As late as May of that year, radios were still forbidden in Virginia Mennonite Conference homes. Too "worldly" I think. But that changed in June with the passing of a new ruling by the Virginia Conference.

Two year earlier in Connellsville, Pennsylvania (1949), Ruth Brunk Stoltzfus pioneered a radio program especially for women. By all counts she was the first Mennonite woman on the airwaves with a regular program. In brainstorming a program name, her husband, Grant, asked her what she hoped to do on the broadcast. Ruth said she just wanted to share ideas, tell stories, and talk "heart to heart." It made a perfect name.

I ended up working for that program in 1975, ghostwriting for Professor Sam's wife, Ella May Miller (who took over from Ruth in 1958).

In its heyday with Ella May, *Heart to Heart* (with Ella May) was airing on 181 stations in its five-minute version, and on 97 stations in a fifteen-minute version (some overlap). The organization had grown a mailing list of more than 25,000 who were eager to receive sorta-schlocky souvenir spoons and hot pads sent to those who wrote in or contributed money. At the program's height, there were also 11,300 fans on a paid subscription list who received printed copies of her content every week.

Both women who headed the program were strong personalities in their own right; I never worked with Ruth, but later in life we enjoyed a sort of mentor/mentee relationship.

This short history of the beginnings of media outreach for Mennonite churches—which grew to a worldwide ministry—is covered in much more depth in Hubert Pellman's *Mennonite Broadcasts: The First 25 Years,* published in 1979. *The Mennonite Hour*, and later the expanded Mennonite Broadcasts, Inc., had humble hometown origins. But underneath was a calling or vision that would later expand to various communication ministries and new media formats.[2]

But of course none of us knew this larger future. I had a lot of just-graduated-from-college greenness when I joined the staff the summer of 1975. Would I be able to do the job? What if I stuttered or misspoke—sometimes a problem for me. Was I plain enough? Should I wear my old traditional head covering? I had pretty much shed my prayer covering while a student at EMC.

During a month at my parents' home before my actual job started, I studied the personnel manual for Mennonite Broadcasts. I learned that women were not allowed to wear slacks to work. Pants were permissible only if they were part of a three-piece suit. Just a top or blouse with slacks would not do. Too revealing, I guess.

Oh well, I thought, "If it doesn't work out, I can always leave in a year or two without damaging my résumé."

For my first day of work in 1975, I wore a pale-yellow safari style jacket with short cuffed sleeves and matching skirt. I made the

---

[2] Note that Mennonites in other localities had started other independent radio broadcasts as early as 1936 when a program called *The Calvary Hour* was started by William (Bill) Detwiler.

outfit myself on Mother's faithful 40s Singer sewing machine. I was accustomed to making most of my own clothes in high school.

As I eagerly walked up the back steps of the former Steele's Furniture building in Harrisonburg I had sometimes noticed as a student at EMC, I was stoked. A real job. My first job after college. They were going to pay me a decent $3.05 an hour and I'd get health insurance, holidays, and vacation time. Pinch, pinch. I wasn't a teacher or a nurse but a secretary. Not exactly the writing I aspired to, but it was a start.

My first day came a day later than planned due to a stomach bug, but no one seemed too rattled by that. As Linda Brubaker—the gal I was replacing—confided: "[Most of the bosses] are out of the office anyway at the every-other-year Mennonite General Assembly."

"Oh, where is it this year?" I queried. As a college student, I was decidedly out of the loop of larger Mennonite-goings-on (having visited "bedside Baptist" too frequently as a junior and senior). But I fondly remembered the 1970 Mennonite Youth Convention I attended in Asheville, North Carolina.

"It's in Eureka, Illinois," Linda stated. Eventually Eureka would be known as the college town of former President Ronald Reagan. The place didn't sound too exciting but somewhere in my psyche was planted a dream: Would I someday be able to travel to a General Assembly on paid time?

But first there was a beast of a copier machine I had to conquer. It occupied a whole small room on the first floor. "It's best to coordinate your trips to the copier to save time," Linda pointed out as we went down the stairs. She also showed me how to fix a jam, where to put money for personal copies, and dozens of other helpful "this is how you survive in an office" tips. She was moving away to get married. Younger than me, she had not completed college, but she filled out my education in helpful ways.

My first immediate boss was Diane Zimmerman Umble, also a young and recently married woman. She knew I had skills and training beyond being a secretary and treated me more like a co-worker than a boss, which was fine by me. She was a writer/producer and assigned to experiment with creative alternative formats for the *Heart to Heart* program and other projects. This led to a little rocking of the boat, she confided, and toward the end of her short tenure, she was just trying to keep the waters calm. Her husband accepted a teaching job at Hesston College in Kansas, so Diane left within two months of my start date.

But in the interim she conveyed to me the confidence I needed to pick up what had been her role as a *Heart to Heart* ghostwriter for Ella May. My main job was secretarial work for *The Mennonite Hour* radio program. I began to feel like I stepped into the organization at just the right time.

When Diane left, my immediate boss became David Thompson, a marketer with an open mind to innovation, including letting a worker be paid and work on two different job levels at the same time. One day not long after I had picked up doing the ghostwriting for *Heart to Heart*, Dave stopped by my desk, which was just outside his office. "I need a writer," Dave grinned, knowing it would be right up my alley. "Ken and I were talking about you working on a promotional package for the special *Heart to Heart* two-minute package Diane worked on before she left."

He let that sink in. My heart started beating faster. "You write pretty good and Ken and I were looking at your portfolio from college. Why don't you try to dummy up a folder and propose copy for the 33 LP size record, which is how we're distributing that package." Thank goodness I understood "dummy up" from my days working on the college paper. My head started brainstorming what the dummy could look like, and about catchy phrases or descriptions I could use to advertise the production.

Dave encouraged me to talk to Lois Hertzler, another younger staff person who was in charge of marketing materials sent to radio stations. So, I set up a time to pick her brain. She told me about the kinds of materials she put into a marketing package. Lois had started at MBI right out of high school and learned from the bottom up, diligently putting her skills at record keeping and organization to whatever project she was assigned. She also knew a lot about what was going on behind the scenes.

And that's how we rolled for the next few months. I attended monthly *Heart to Heart* discussion groups with different local women who were invited to help Ella May brainstorm ideas for upcoming programs. It was my first experience getting paid to sit in meetings and just talk. This was work? The speaker would write three or four programs a month, and I was to do one week's worth of programs, which spelled her for her other responsibilities. She was a popular speaker for women's groups and was often on the road.

I don't remember who suggested the idea of *Heart to Heart* having a program on the art of quilting, but Ella May seemed to warm to the idea. This traditional form of folk art was regaining popularity at the time. I quickly volunteered to write on that topic for my first ghostwritten script. My Aunt Susie Roth, a quilting maestra, swiftly came to mind. "I have an aunt who makes more quilts than anyone I know," I said, my mind churning with ideas. "I could write to her and see if she could help me come up with a simple quilt pattern that we could offer to listeners," I speculated.

I could see Ella May was responding well to the idea with an agreeable nod. Another woman in the group mentioned some other local quilters she knew who would likely be happy to be interviewed for the program. I swiftly jotted down names. I started harnessing my skills from college newspaper days on how to go about writing an article. Researching and collecting the content for a radio program was not so different.

But could I truly take my thoughts and research and make the writing believable for a longtime speaker/writer for the show, to voice as her own material? The topic was certainly not a controversial one, which was fine by me. If I first loved being a writer because of bylines, there isn't normally any credit given to a ghostwriter, as the name implies. But as a staff writer, this wasn't a big issue: I was beginning to feel part of a team of people working together for a larger goal.

I have to chuckle now about the letter I sent to my Aunt Susie, which sounds a little like sixth grade:

> Hi! Did you know that I am working here at MBI? Well, I am and the reason I'm writing to you is because I'd like a little information from you to help me on one of my assignments.

Aunt Susie agreeably got on board and sent some sample patches by mail with a description about how to put together several fairly advanced patterns. I decided on a pinwheel quilt for a free pattern for listeners who might write in, the simplest pattern I knew. I also interviewed my sister's mother-in-law by mail, and two local women by phone. We incorporated all their best tips and I typed it (long before computers) and ran off photocopies of the pattern on legal-size paper.

To pretty much everyone's amazement, especially my own, the requests for that simple Xeroxed quilt pattern from *Heart to Heart* began to trickle—and then *pour* in. The mail count was up for weeks. I think the total number of pieces of mail was close to two thousand, a record, if I recollect correctly, for a single program. It was hard not to take it personally, but I was excited and felt like I had sealed up something: my place on the staff maybe?

In November, I read about a conference put together by the Evangelical Women's Caucus, which was sort of a feminist organization, happening in Washington, D.C. As a writer for the program and knowing the board wanted our women's program to appeal more broadly, I approached my boss Dave saying the conference would maybe be a good continuing education opportunity. He gave the green light and newbie that I was, I set about making my travel plans to get to D.C. without asking for anyone's guidance or advice. I felt it would be easier to use public transportation than drive myself into the city with my old '66 family Chevy.

So I bought a Greyhound ticket (classy travel). After arriving in the city, I hailed a taxi to the 4-H Center for the site of the conference. The conference was eye opening, with the keynote speaker being Virginia Ramey Mollenkott, an English literature professor, undoubtedly the most powerful female preacher I had ever heard.

One workshop I went to related to single women. We discussed the issue of dealing with sexual feelings and desires as singles and shared our personal status.

I was 23 and feeling (in that era) that I was reaching an age where many of my friends were already married. Many girls in my high school class had already gotten married the summer we graduated from high school. As I shared my story, I added that I had just gotten engaged.

One woman immediately took me on, but not unkindly. "Well, *your* struggles will soon be over!" she pointed out. I wondered if I shouldn't have attended that workshop but I just smiled and shrugged my shoulders.

The conference helped expand my horizons and I was glad I went. I also sensed my bosses were happy for me to take the initiative to grow in my job. What did Ella May think about my little foray to the national capital? I'll never know and was not given to pushing boundaries. I think that kept her comfortable with me and my ghostwriting. She sometimes edited my writing, but not much. She was the matriarch of the program: not only her voice, but her face appeared on many of the newsletters and program literature. Among Mennonite women especially, she was a household name, voice, and face.

I heard enough insider gossip at the office that some on the board thought it was time for *Heart to Heart* and our other programs to stop sending out gimmicky mailing list builders and fundraising pulls. They also expressed a sentiment that a speaker who was more open to women being encouraged to use their gifts—beyond homemaking—would be appreciated. But to my knowledge, no one ever asked her to resign.

Ella May clearly taught that a woman's first place was in the home and only out of necessity should she work outside of the home. If someone asked Ella May about her own employment, she was always quick to mention that her children were in school by the time she became speaker on *Heart to Heart* and she considered it a calling or ministry, not a job. Overall, she and other Christians at the time believed women should not work outside the home. I had no inkling that this kind of more conservative Christian hard line on the place of women would come back to bite me much later on.

Perhaps an organizational financial mistake was also made by not fully recognizing the pulling power of a strong radio voice. An early "Mennonite Beth Moore," for instance? Was it so wrong to have a popular speaker, especially one as dedicated as Ella May?

Ella May actually helped to pioneer the work of Mennonite Broadcasts toward shorter programming to fit the needs and technology of the times. The 5-minute daily program came about in 1962, before Mennonite Broadcasts had experimented with *any* shorter programming. As Ella May traveled and came in contact with station personnel, they asked for shorter programs because people no longer sat down and listened to the radio in long time blocks.

Ella May said her worst moment came at the height of the women's movement in 1975 when she was picketed before she was to speak at a women's meeting in Pennsylvania. The National Organization of Women had gotten word that she would be there and protested her appearance in the morning. Ella May said she was naïve in asking to dialogue with the leaders, who were on entirely different wavelengths than Ella May. "I told them I'm not against women working. I just wanted to keep homemaking top priority." They didn't come back, though, when she spoke at the church that evening.

Ella May eventually sensed in 1976 that she was at a different place than the Mennonite Broadcasts, Inc., board with her perspectives on women and graciously said it was time for her to move on. This was pretty much at the height of the program's popularity. Her gift of being dogmatic but approachable, with a keen sense of her target audience still makes successful radio personalities.

Years later I had the opportunity to do an interview with Ella May reflecting on her years with *Heart to Heart* for an article in the *Christian Living* magazine that Mennonite Publishing House published. As she looked back, Ella May gave all the credit to God, not unexpectedly. "The Lord prepared me," she framed her role. "I never thought I had any special gifts, never thought I'd amount to anything. I simply told the Lord, 'I'm available.'"

Then she went on, "The reason the Lord used *Heart to Heart* so successfully was I focused on a target audience, and focused on just one woman. That made it more personable." Incidentally, that is excellent media strategy, especially in radio, focusing on one person or an archetype persona as we would say today. "I didn't recite Bible verses, but used biblical principles. Theology doesn't mean a thing unless it is understood in practical terms. I marvel that thousands were touched; homes and marriages were saved. We received many testimonies."

Ella May shared how one letter came from a businessman who related how he had been on a work trip. He said he was about to ask for a call girl for the night. He heard the *Heart to Heart* program, with Ella May saying that God's design was for one man to be married to one woman. "I had never been exposed to that idea. Instead of getting a call girl, I went to my room and called my wife." Today we would say "sex worker" instead of "call girl" but we can certainly laud any program or message that inspires a guy to call home instead of having a one-night (or hour) encounter.

Rather than seeking a career, Ella May carved out her very own niche as a servant/mission worker in North America. In her interview she shared some reflections on her isolation as a newlywed mission couple with husband Sam (my former professor) in Argentina. They were sent there without any orientation at all in those days. She noted that was the last era in which mission workers did not receive orientation—and a good reminder of how critical it is as well as ongoing moral support.

Ella May not only experienced what she termed a nervous breakdown, but a difficult delivery of her first baby where she almost died. She had to stay in a clinic for 2½ months, and her sister flew to Argentina to help them out. Ella May's own mother died when she was ten. She went through her teen years without a mom—a hole no one could fill. This also led to her taking on "mothers" as a ministry.

• • • • •

My dual work with *Heart to Heart* and *The Mennonite Hour* also took me back to an earlier era, which I experienced firsthand as a child. There was a Sunday evening event at our church in the latter 50s, when Sunday evening services were a bit less formal than Sunday morning.

The atmosphere in our very plain sanctuary at North Goshen Mennonite Church burbled with excited chatter. A tour bus trekking *The Mennonite Hour* choir and quartet to mostly Mennonite churches all across the U.S. and Canada was parked at our church! The enthusiastic crowd was gathering to see and hear a mid-50s phenomenon: a radio preacher and a four-part a cappella choir from a program they frequently listened to on Sunday mornings as they got ready for church. This was before most Mennonite homes had TV of any kind. I'm sure the church was packed. And I'm also fairly certain that radio pastor B. Charles Hostetter addressed the crowd that night. Hostetter, and later speaker David Augsburger were household names across the Mennonite Church because of *The Mennonite Hour* radio program and in some wider Christian circles.

The "home" office of the *Mennonite Hour* program at the time was a 3-story, 20-room headquarters fronting on historic Route 11 in Harrisonburg, Virginia (different building than the one I would eventually work in). My family had once visited there on vacation.

For some reason the part that sticks in my mind from that tour was an office filled with cubby holes where various Home Bible Study lessons were kept in orderly fashion. The follow-up department sent the lessons out to those responding to offers to enroll in free Bible study courses. The whole office smelled like freshly printed paper.

• • • • •

Fast forward 20 years from that early concert. I gradually connected the dots that the same *Mennonite Hour* radio program I had a tiny taste of at my home church in Indiana was the organization that had hired me. The ministry was now housed in a different building, along Route 42 in Harrisonburg, next door to Eastern Mennonite College.

What does a *Mennonite Hour* secretary do? My duties included receiving taped messages (on old reel-to-reel tapes) and threading them onto a large tape recorder stored in my office. Then I timed the message with a stopwatch, while focusing on the speaker's theme. That helped me find appropriate hymns to add to the message. I could pick from a repertoire of hundreds of pieces of recorded music in our "*Mennonite Hour* tape library," mostly lovely a cappella.

I also created and kept a production schedule up to date, sent reports to a clearance center on what music we were using (so the composers/text writers could be paid for use of their work on the radio), and processed mail from readers.

When the programs were assembled by the audio engineer, I gathered an "auditioning" committee, which drove about a mile to our studio—a converted chicken house! We listened to the final product to check for any missed flubs or false starts that may have been inadvertently overlooked. It often seemed like the auditioning committee wasn't satisfied it was doing its job unless it found at least one error, or *something* that could have been done better.

To make up for my overall lack of training in this area, I signed up to audit a class at nearby Madison College (now James Madison

University) regarding history of radio communications. The only formal communications courses I had been able to take at EMC were feature writing and creative writing. Journalism and media studies were not quite a thing yet at EMC.

One day after our auditioning committee had picked apart a small error at our studio, the engineer at the time, Larry Heatwole, studied those of us in the master control room. Typically, if it was necessary to cut out an extra "s" or an erroneous pause, he spliced the tape by hand with a razor blade, and then taped it back together. A smile flickered across his face.

"I'll tell you the engineering secret that Abe (Rittenhouse) taught me," Larry's eyes were mischievous, "if you promise not to tell other audition groups."

The three of us on the team were all ears, nodding in conspiracy. "Once in a while I've been known to leave in a noticeable flub on purpose." He allowed his confession to sink in. That didn't sound like our perfectionist engineer. "It's to distract the listening committee from an unfixable minor mispronunciation or the like," Larry admitted. He then finished his story telling how one time either Abe or he, I can't remember now, actually caught flak from a radio station for forgetting to fix a bad flub that an engineer had left in for this very reason. A big oops!

*Former headquarters for Mennonite Broadcasts, which Melodie's family toured in 1966. The headquarters were once a popular tour site for Mennonites visiting the Shenandoah Valley.*

*Ella May Miller, speaker on the* Heart to Heart *radio program. Melodie served as a ghostwriter for about a year and a half.*

*In the background on the right, notice the reel-to-reel tape recorder the producer used for listening to* Mennonite Hour *sermons and choosing fitting hymns for the program.*

# THE MENNONITE HOUR

EXPLORING THE RELEVANCY OF CHRISTIAN FAITH WITH BILL BRECKBILL

## the speaker...

As a seasoned pastor, scholar and counselor, Bill Breckbill is especially well-equipped to prod persons to deeper Christian dedication and service.

Bill is a husband and the father of four children. He has served in the ministry since 1955, and presently pastors the Preston Mennonite Church at Cambridge, Ontario.

With on-target illustrations and warmth, Breckbill's messages relate faith to job, family, and neighbors. He helps listeners to greater understanding of what it means to *be* the church.

*Bill Breckbill*

## program themes

- Relating in love
- Living out the message of the Gospels
- Members of Christ's family
- Marriage and family life
- Consistent Christianity
- Being a blessing
- Congregational life

## a community witness

*The Mennonite Hour* presents a much-needed challenge to persons to live a meaningful and useful life. It helps to extend the witness of the congregation in the community. And, it adds prestige to the religious programming of radio stations.

## follow-up activities

*The Mennonite Hour* is backed by caring persons responding to needs and concerns of listeners who write for counsel. Special home Bible studies and booklets are offered free to listeners, as a part of the follow-up program.

*Brochure featuring new* Mennonite Hour *speaker Bill Breckbill after a long run by speaker David Augsburger.*

CHAPTER 3

# Just Who Are Your Mennonites in Congress, Anyway?

One day my overall supervisor, David Thompson, stopped at my desk and said something like: "How would you like to take minutes as our *Heart to Heart* Task Force debates and discusses the future of women's programming?"

I sniffed the opportunity to travel behind his question.

When Ella May decided to retire in my first year of employment, I was a little surprised. But apparently it was a step Ella May had been mulling for some time. The board moved quickly to appoint a task force, which would work at not only securing a new speaker, but likely a whole new direction for the program.

Who would have thought that gaining a small reputation for thorough minutes would open such doors? My head reeled. As a novice staff member, ordinarily I would not have been privy to insider secrets of boardrooms and a task force hashing out how to make a major programming change. But I was single, didn't have a family, and thus a little freer to travel out of town than the program's regular secretary, Evelyn Sauder. She was superb at all she did, by the way, and knew and used real shorthand. I was in awe.

My mind raced as Dave described tentative plans. He said the task force would mostly meet off-location in places like Crystal City complex (at that time a hotel, restaurant, and meeting rooms near

Washington, D.C.). And there were also plans to meet at a church in the heart of Mennoniteville in eastern Pennsylvania. Yes, thank you, I would be happy to take minutes.

A month or so later I passed through the lobby at Crystal City, tingling with anticipation, I was awed by the huge chandeliers hanging there. The discussions ranged from hearing some task force members say it was due time (late 1970s) to leave behind a program that still emphasized that a woman's main place was in the home—and probably not behind the pulpit.

Some administrators and board were also somewhat wary that the radio program sometimes functioned too much as a celebrity fan club. But of course the bottom line swelled when books by Ella May grew in popularity. One book, *A Woman in Her Home*, surpassed 200,000 books in print. That kind of reach is what it takes to make a successful radio or TV program.

Christian radio and TV programming was just coming into its heyday of evangelical fundraising in the late 70s, before some of the scandals of the later 80s took place. I loved being a fly on the wall of those meeting rooms as I took detailed minutes, hearing things I knew I couldn't share outside the meeting space (except maybe now after a time and epoch lapse of 40-50 years!).

Ella May tried to talk her office colleague, Eva Stauffer, (both in their early 60s) into retiring, too. Eva answered most of the mail Ella May received—especially that which required a more personal or counseling response. Eva and Ella May were true office cohorts—both wearing only dresses or skirts to work and both faithfully donning Mennonite coverings for the three-times-a-week staff assemblies and prayer meetings.

But Eva did not take Ella May's nudge to also retire. Eva worked another couple years until a heart attack weakened her. She then resigned for health reasons. She was a gem: dedicated, thorough, and caring in what she did. I always admired how Eva resisted the push to retire with Ella May. I also owe Ella May and her husband Sam a debt of gratitude for the steps that led to my employment and opportunities.

• • • • •

Our overall record with stations was one of respect and high marks: well-executed programming that never tried to raise funds on air.

Eventually my position was expanded to include not only doing the secretarial work for *The Mennonite Hour* program, but to serve as producer, which carried slightly more authority and clout on staff. Years later I had my own secretary and asked that her position be split 50/50 with secretarial work and administrative oversight of an area of our work. I was told that according to the human resources department of Mennonite Board of Missions (MBM), our larger "ruling" entity at the time, no one was allowed to work on two pay levels—even if it made sense! I was glad that policy was not enforced when I first started out.

As a producer, I now met about once a week with either the director of English (language) media, Dave Thompson, or Ken Weaver as executive director. With young adult producer Diane Umble gone from our staff, Ken approached me one day with a project proposal. He wondered if I would be open to produce some radio spots for youth from Mennonite churches to place on their local stations.

"Well, that's certainly a market we're not hitting now," I agreed, stalling as I mulled what he was saying.

"A few years back, Jim Fairfield was a creative powerhouse working with Dave Augsburger on some of our more innovative radio efforts," Ken added. "He still lives around here and I'm guessing we could talk him into working with you on a new series."

"That would be cool to work with Jim," I responded. "I'm not too up on today's radio scene for kids but I'm certainly game to take that on." I took a deep breath. How exciting. My adrenaline was running.

I stopped in to talk with my co-worker Lois about what she knew about working with Fairfield. She was enthusiastic, mentioning how David Augsburger and Fairfield had brainstormed and produced the creative *Greatest Week in History* radio programs. Those were mock newscasts imagining what the triumphal entry of Christ, the last supper, the arrest, trial, and crucifixion would have sounded like on a modern-day radio news program. Stations used these holiday broadcasts each Easter, and Jim and Dave both were part of that success. I knew one of Jim's daughters from my college days, and had seen him around the office, too. He still worked as a freelancer producing marketing and jingles for businesses.

We soon scheduled a meet up with Jim. One of the ideas that emerged was to take Proverbs as a source of wisdom for young *and* old and play with the various ideas. Someone suggested multimedia products to go along with the radio spots such as posters for youth to put up at their churches, ads promoting the radio series in papers, and even slides for TV stations to use. Jim and I had fun conceiving several ideas and both of us wrote the spots. We then lined up a seasoned radio announcer from two-hours distant Roanoke, to do the voiceovers. The spots ended up sounding very professional.

Some were whimsical or meant to be lighter:

> "It's better to eat soup with someone you love, than steak with someone you hate."
>
> "What'd you say?"
>
> "I said it's better to eat soup with someone you love, than steak with someone you hate."
>
> "Oh, okay."
>
> A proverb for today, from the Mennonite churches.

One of the heavier spots conveyed: "What's more important? Having things or having friends?" The proverb quoted in this spot was "Riches disappear as though they had the wings of a bird" (Proverbs. 23:4, *Living Bible*), and ended with the tag "Caring about people adds up to worthwhile living." The spot was spot on but the poster that portrayed it was the most embarrassing artwork I ever signed off on. It included a poorly drawn male head looking at a bag of money that actually had a dollar sign on it, to illustrate this message. Not a proud product or moment, but it rolled out along with better visuals as well.

Our goal was to introduce them at the Mennonite Church youth and adult conventions to be held—for the first time, I think—at the same location and dates: the Rocky Mountains in Colorado. It didn't take me long to set a goal of going to the convention—just two years after I started my job. It wasn't hard to talk Ken into it, and I planned a seminar introducing the radio spot series to youth.

Then I learned my parents and one sister were also going—Mom and Dad as chauffeurs for the youth group from their church (yea Mom and Dad for volunteering in retirement). My athletic sister helped with the recreation program for youth at the convention.

And shoot, I speculated, if I was giving one youth seminar, why not make it doubly worthwhile by offering to do a second on a personal issue and bridge I had recently gone over? That is: What to do if you found yourself in a romantic relationship with someone of another Christian denomination, and your parents weren't sure if they could go along with it.

Yes, we're talking just different "denominations," not *religions*. In those days, it was just a bit unusual for Mennonite youth to marry outside of the church—and in some areas, the ideal was that you found someone in your own congregation to love and marry. At my parents' church in Indiana at that time, I recall one couple talking about how when they married from differing Mennonite churches, it disappointed their parents somewhat. (I think—and hope—the parents got over it.)

The seminar was fully packed out with some kids sitting on the floor. I was just a few years older than these juniors and seniors in high school, and many were dealing with differences much wider than a Mennonite marrying a Methodist. The sharing got really personal in the after-seminar conversations.

These experiences helped me realize how much I loved speaking to and interacting with groups in such a setting—something I never planned for or realized as a student myself. I loved that this job allowed me to explore new avenues and opportunities. I give credit to the environment in the organization. It seemed primed to nurture growth and not stagnation.

However, when I look now at the small newspaper ads and posters we produced for those youth groups to use in announcing and promoting the "Proverbs" radio spots in their communities, I shake my head wondering where was the art director on these? Oh yes, he was an acquaintance I knew from my days working at the local public service television station. He was the only graphic artist I knew and again, I didn't know the ins and outs of our organization enough to have just asked the staff person who usually worked with outside graphic designers to do that for this project as well.

I'd made it to producer. And I still had a lot to learn.

We attempted to put our learnings to work in a sequel with "Proverb Series 2." The themes were worthwhile for any generation: how to take criticism without exploding; the struggle for power; when everything goes wrong at once; what to do if you're not a born leader.

• • • • •

The woman eventually selected by the task force and board to take over women's programming was Margaret Foth of Clarence, New York. She had a master's in education, and experience teaching in nearby Buffalo. But it was her church work and family interests, lovely voice, and commitment to the Anabaptist Christian lifestyle and values—even when they were unpopular—that attracted the task force to Margaret's résumé. She also had a major interest in theater and drama and had done writing along those lines.

"We want someone actively involved in raising a family but far enough through the process to have some perspective," I recall one task force member saying, likely also thinking of the practical aspects of not needing daycare if they had older children. Margaret's oldest son Bob had just started at the College of William and Mary in Williamsburg, Virginia; their three daughters Ellen, Mary, and Jan were still in high school or grade school. Margaret commuted weekends to her home in New York state for the first nine months or so, until the rest of the family could move to Harrisonburg. Eventually, her husband, Don, took a job first as controller at local radio station WSVA, and later at EMC. It was unusual in that time for a family to move for a wife's job, something Margaret was happy to point out.

After a lengthy process brainstorming and testing program names, the task force and Margaret landed on the name *Your Time,* for the program. "We want this to be a time of reflection and space for women to reflect and process their lives," one task force member put it. The five-minute daily program began airing on approximately 90 stations that had used *Heart to Heart.* I continued being a ghostwriter for the new speaker one week each month.

Margaret described her target audience as "whoever is listening to radio—which may include men," and she brought her interests in many social issues as well as her people-oriented personality to the program. Her weekly subjects included many aspects of family living, including discipline, which is guiding and loving; families caring for children with special needs; welcoming international guests into our homes; developing habits of self-care; and choosing simplicity.

She sought out persons to regularly interview on the program, so that listeners heard lived experiences as well as a variety of voices. One of her interviewees was Alice Parker, the famous composer for the Shaw Chorale who was living with the grief and stress of suddenly losing her husband: "Every step felt like a cement block was attached to my shoe," Alice said. Others included Mennonite educator Alta Mae Erb on the nurture of children; Presbyterian pastor Ben Weir after his return from being held hostage, reflecting on forgiving those who had abused him; and a man on a hunger strike protesting the sale of arms to the Sandinistas (political party in Nicaragua).

"The peace witness was very important to me," said Margaret. Her emphasis came through strongly enough several times that some of her more conservative religious stations dropped the program. "My understanding of faith is that all of my life, whatever I do, living and relating to people, is what I'm called to do. To share that kind of perspective is an important part of mission," Margaret stated.

Margaret's position also included accepting invitations to speak to many organizations and churches. She traveled often to churches in Virginia for an evening program and other times for a weekend program in Pennsylvania, Ohio, New York, and even Ontario.

By her own admission, her biggest challenge through the years was "How to get the next program done. It was a real discipline to get it done in the [weekly] time frame."

• • • • •

One of the passions I carried for a while on staff was helping to educate Mennonite church families and members regarding how much violence had infiltrated all of our lives through the medium of television.

In the late 1970s, just twenty years removed from the 50s heyday of the first real television entertainment, people absorbed television without much thought or critique of how incredibly influential it had become in their lives and world. Some favorite shows of that era: *Father Knows Best*, *I Love Lucy*, *Lassie*, and *Gunsmoke*. Leave *Gunsmoke* off the list if you grew up Mennonite. We were not allowed to watch anything that had bloodshed, especially via guns.

Sometime around 1977 some religious groups were becoming increasingly aware that their children and teenagers were being sucked into watching television for four to six hours a day. In many homes the television was always on as background noise for families, full-time mothers, and retirees.

And what messages were all of us absorbing in those untold hours? Murder and mayhem of course, with plenty of dripping blood. Concerned advocates organized a comprehensive Television Awareness Training (TAT)[3] program consisting of a textbook/workbook, and reels of film with specific TV samples. The films were like old-fashioned movie film (before videos or video projectors, before DVDs, before YouTube).

One of those involved in planning and directing the overall program was my original boss at Mennonite Broadcasts, Diane Umble, who had moved on to be director of a similar media office for the General Conference Mennonite Church, a sister denomination to Mennonites (later united). When I learned of a seminar for potential Television Awareness Training leaders in nearby Richmond, Virginia, I approached our director, Ken. "You've heard about the Television Awareness Training workshops that Diane Umble and others we know have helped to organize?" I asked in my weekly one-on-one with him. Ken appeared intrigued. "Would you want us to get involved in this program as a service for Mennonite churches?"

"Go on," Ken urged.

"I heard there's a training weekend going on in Richmond, and two women locally from the Church of the Brethren are participating. We could share transportation," I added, thinking that might make the prospect more affordable.

In addition to our former colleague Diane being involved, I

---

3 TAT was developed by the United Methodist Church, Church of the Brethren, and Media Action Research Center, Inc. More on this movement can be found at the Center for Media Literacy online at medialit.com.

knew Ken was acquainted with Stewart Hoover of the Church of the Brethren, and others from the National Council of Churches Communications Commission (NCCCC), a group that also endorsed this new effort.

Ken did not hesitate—he was always more than willing to give the nod to new opportunities to serve the church, and to align ourselves with the newest and next thing in media. He didn't mind us going out on a limb to try something new.

The training was eye-opening and I soon became a certified leader. We began to offer TAT classes or workshops in local Virginia churches. To save dollars, I shared the trunk of films and materials with a Church of the Brethren leader in our area, Ramona Pence, who later became an ordained pastor. (That vintage trunk, which held those films still graces my laundry room, holding a beloved large plant, in case you wanted to know.)

I loved this circuit, even though I always felt a little guilty preaching to parents how they needed to set boundaries on how much TV their children could watch, since I was not a parent yet. Again, this was long before other "screens" had addicted us.

Word-of-mouth about these workshops spread, and I was invited to probably a dozen or more Mennonite churches in our local area, including one church that dedicated a 13-week study to the material. Every Sunday morning my husband and I went to their Sunday school hour instead of our own. The materials were absorbing (watching television, after all) and people had no trouble contributing to the discussions. Everyone watched or had opinions on various shows, characters, and the underlying messages that programs and advertisements were sending out.

Eventually I was invited to lead a weekend retreat for Church of the Brethren youth in one of our Virginia districts, held at a camp in southeastern Virginia. I was thrilled for the opportunity, and being not long out of high school and college myself, the weekend was a good success except for one mishap.

My sleeping quarters were at the top of a bunk (I don't recall if I had to share the room or not) but on one of my trips up or down, I experienced a very bad fall, which left my back super sore the next day. I also experienced an unusually heavy period. I speculated I may very well have had a miscarriage—perhaps prompted by my fall from the bunk ladder.

TAT ran its course and eventually I stopped getting invitations to speak to groups or churches on that topic, but it awakened in me the enjoyment of speaking to groups. I always told people I stopped doing seminars on being careful television viewers when my own three daughters eventually came along, and I learned what a convenient babysitter TV could be.

• • • • •

Margaret and I became friends as well as co-workers. Twenty or so years my senior, I envied her master's degree. Did I need one, too? But at least I had almost two years' experience working in the office and media by the time she moved her family to Harrisonburg. She always treated me more like an equal colleague than an underling—bouncing ideas, gripes, and joys off me.

We especially enjoyed traveling adventures. In the early 80s we participated in an inspiring five days in Nashville at a training event organized by the United Methodist communications organization called Bushel Basket Workshop. It focused on video production, and was geared to women in media-related vocations. We were from diverse backgrounds and faith groups: Catholic, Methodist, Mennonite, Jewish, Baptist. Denominations were just getting into using the new video medium to create curriculums, discussion starters, outreach materials, training resources, and reports.

The workshop was a week of bonding with like-minded souls. We watched one young sister, in this case an actual nun, shed her headgear—yes the coif and band—and get her hair cut and styled that week. Her transformation was amazing, and not unlike when Mennonite women, such as my mother, first got their long hair cut.

The week was an immense privilege of stepping outside my routine work to mix with many wonderful women. We were placed on teams cutting across faith lines, and together produced videos using semi-professional video cameras and simple editing tools on the cameras. Our group—very original we were—used "You Light Up My Life" as the theme song for our pitifully painful production. I completely forget what kind of visuals we created, or the story we told.

On another trip, Dale Stoltzfus, a pastor in New York City's South Bronx and our board president, invited a small group of staff including newer speakers Art McPhee and Margaret to experience what ministry looked like in the inner city of the late 70s. He was passionate about the hurts and needs away from more traditional Mennonite rural communities. "The staff need to meet the people I rub shoulders with every day," Dale explained as he pushed the board to pay for a three-day exposure.

After a six-hour-drive, we stepped outside the office station wagon onto one of New York City's well-used and garbage strewn sidewalks. I slowly took a deep breath. Ah—that aroma of diesel buses—an unusual scent to enjoy, to be sure. But it transported me from the rural life I had grown up with (and still mostly live in the Shenandoah Valley), to the hardscrabble busy streets of a huge city. This was before the Bronx's well-known revival and recovery from urban blight, which began later in the 80s. There were still many burned-out buildings. The sights were startlingly oppressive and depressing.

Dale had arranged interviews and inside tours of several Mennonite helping organizations in the city, and Ken set up meetings with others working in media or at the "God Box" (475 Riverside Drive), a 19-story building that housed a concentration of religious organizations. We met with the area's church council, toured WNBC, a Hope Center for alcohol and drug addicts, Norman Vincent Peale's church, and visited the production set of the Today Show. We drank in culture, observed the crass commercialism of Times Square, the plight of the homeless, and the sad prospects of living in the Projects, (dare I mention treating ourselves to several evening Broadway plays). It was eye and mind-opening.

• • • • •

Later several of us took another jaunt to New York City. Ken had pushed me to arrange voice coaching for our two main speakers, Art and Margaret. He wanted us to have an outsider's objective look at their style and content. Ken always strived to have the staff produce award-winning, excellent material.

So we were able to meet with Himan Brown, a producer of some renown for the radio mystery program *CBS Mystery Theater.* This was arranged through the National Academy of Television Arts and Sciences (which gives out the Emmy Awards) and the National Council of Churches (NCC) communications division (which Mennonite Media participated in without being actual members).

*CBS Mystery Theater* was a radio favorite from roughly 1974-1982 with a cult following like NPR's current *Wait, Wait, Don't Tell Me!* radio program. The studio for *CBS Mystery Theater* (old shows are still online) also had seats for an audience to observe the recordings, complete with zany sound effects such as a scary creaky door, breaking glass, and spooky howling wind.

As Brown debriefed us after listening to our program tapes, he didn't spend a lot of time nitpicking the productions. "You're doing fine, just fine. Ah, maybe a few tweaks, but what I want you to look at is how *you can reach more people* with what you're doing. How many stations are you on?"

We told him, perhaps padding the numbers by an extra station or two that were maybe not actually airing the program anymore.

"Well, you need to reach out to your Mennonite congressmen

or women to reach more people, have more impact," he said with his terrific Yiddish twang. "Who are they anyway, give me some names," he urged.

We looked at each other, a bit dumbfounded. "Oh we're a very small religious group, I don't think we have any people in Congress," Ken stammered quickly and we stifled our blushes.

These kinds of trips and continuing education were a luxury, I realize now. In my later career after a merger with Herald Press book and curriculum publishers, anything but the most critical travel to church meetings and conferences were ever a possibility, owing to lack of budget. And such trips became mostly reserved for department heads, not often other employees.

• • • • •

Speaking of books, it was the early 80s that I began to dream of becoming a published author myself. My ears perked up in meetings when the director of Choice Books bookrack ministry, Paul Yoder, spoke with Margaret about how she could build her following. Earlier speakers (Ella May Miller, B. Charles Hostetter, David Augsburger) had produced bestselling books out of their material. This of course was at a different time in publishing when there were not anywhere close to the number of books or book authors as there are today.

"The best thing to do rather than compile a whole nonfiction book is to first come up with a book proposal and shop it around to publishers," Paul explained. At that time an agent wasn't so crucial and religious publishers especially still waded through many book manuscripts sent in "over the transom." (According to Wikipedia, "the phrase 'over the transom' refers to works submitted for publication without being solicited. The image evoked is of a writer tossing a manuscript through the open window over the door of the publisher's office. In architecture, a transom is a transverse horizontal structural beam or bar, or a crosspiece separating a door from a window above it.")

Could I do that? Not toss a manuscript over a door, but write a book. Could I take my long dream of being a published author and begin to concretize it?

Paul was ticking through a specific list of how to put together a book proposal: write a sample chapter or two, construct a complete outline with short paragraph descriptions of each chapter, write a bang-up query letter telling the purpose of the book and why the book would sell better than any other on the market on that topic, and compose a sizzling author bio.

I could hardly wait to get home that night and start ruffling through my files and journals to think about putting together my first book proposal. I was only working about 60 percent time at the office after our first child, Michelle, was born. After dinner and putting her safely to bed, I began and wrote feverishly, either longhand or on my old manual typewriter. So I made this a strictly off-work project. Such efforts at home often ended up giving me experience or expertise for projects at work.

I went to bed excited and soon realized I was unable to sleep. I got back up and worked a few more hours until I thought I could finally go to sleep.

Paul also proposed turning radio scripts into newspaper columns; his previous job had been as the manager of a small shopper newspaper in Ohio. He talked about how papers were often looking for uplifting material to plunk into empty spaces not filled with advertising. Perhaps Margaret's programs could be recycled into a small print column and function as an audience builder and income stream for the program. But how to plan and write radio programs, write a book, and oh yeah, repurpose her radio scripts into shorter columns?

Margaret was interested and eager but perhaps overwhelmed with some of the expectations being tossed her way. Eventually she was able to write *Life Is Too Short to Miss Today* out of some of her radio programs, and was successfully published in 1985 by Zondervan.

The overall mindset of the organization's staff and board kept me interested. There was a bent for creativity and openness for new opportunities however they came. My own brain and spirit kept spinning. This job was challenging enough. Finding another job in a couple years rarely crossed my mind.

How do you really find what you are to do and be in life anyway? Is it a discovery made as a 16-year-old in a smelly chicken house? Is it learning something new about yourself? Is it feeling a nudge, hearing a comment by a teacher or pastor's wife about your gifts, seeing an open door, or feeling a surge of excitement and challenge in your bones as you approach a job or project?

I loved that there was a mindset favoring innovation in the organizational DNA of Mennonite Broadcasts, Inc. The organization maintained these mostly entrepreneurial bones years down the line.

After all, it had gotten its start when college students in 1951 first approached local radio station WSVA (still a popular major local station in the Shenandoah Valley today), asking if they could present a weekly program of a cappella "Mennonite" music.

More opportunities seemed to lay ahead, although the ugly cloud of budget shortfalls was also always on the horizon.

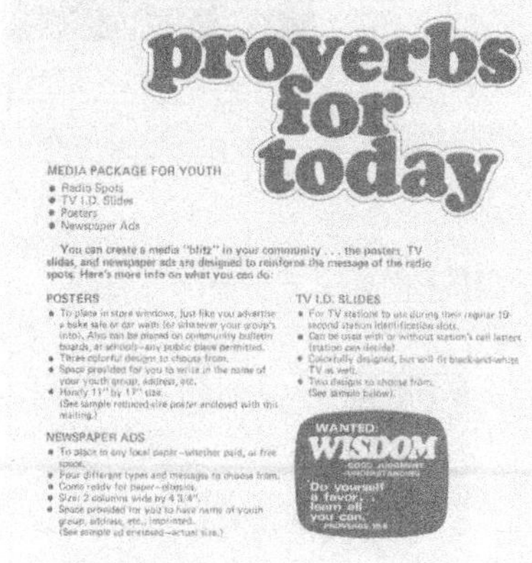
proverbs for today

MEDIA PACKAGE FOR YOUTH

- Radio Spots
- TV I.D. Slides
- Posters
- Newspaper Ads

You can create a media "blitz" in your community . . . the posters, TV slides, and newspaper ads are designed to reinforce the message of the radio spots. Here's more info on what you can do:

POSTERS

- To place in store windows, just like you advertise a bake sale or car wash (or whatever your group's into). Also can be placed on community bulletin boards, at schools—any public place permitted.
- Three colorful designs to choose from.
- Space provided for you to write in the name of your youth group, address, etc.
- Handy 11" by 17" size. (See sample reduced-size poster enclosed with this mailing.)

NEWSPAPER ADS

- To place in any local paper—whether paid, or free space.
- Four different types and messages to choose from.
- Come ready for paper—glossies.
- Size: 2 columns wide by 4 3/4".
- Space provided for you to have name of youth group, address, etc., imprinted. (See sample ad enclosed—actual size.)

TV I.D. SLIDES

- For TV stations to use during their regular 10-second station identification slots.
- Can be used with or without station's call letters (station can decide)
- Colorfully designed, but will fit black-and-white TV as well.
- Two designs to choose from. (See sample below).



(DETACH HERE)

## What's More Important?

HAVING THINGS?
or
HAVING FRIENDS?

"Riches disappear as though they had the wings of a bird." PROVERBS 23:4, LB

**CARING ABOUT PEOPLE ADDS UP TO WORTHWHILE LIVING**

proverbs for today

**MEDIA FOR YOUTH**

Here are public service radio spots especially for the youth in your audience.

Kids today are questioning values and often shaping their own new ideals that make a lot of sense. These radio spots are designed to encourage kids to think through their motives and actions, and then to hang onto their ideals as they face adult pressures.

The ***target audience*** for these spots is YOUTH, senior high age through three years after high school. (Average age range 16-22 years.) This age group is beginning to exercise their independence from parents and think about their own goals for life.

Your station can encourage kids to think for themselves through these public service spots.

## Radio Spots

**Package and use:**

- 14 spots, 20, 30, and 60 seconds in length
- music is upbeat, strong contemporary and country/western sounds
- designed to fit the fast-paced format of today's stations
- some spots end with a write-in offer for a free copy of ***Living Proverbs***
- stations can use any time, not dated
- available free to stations for sustaining (public service) time
- sponsor's tag can be added if desired by local group

*Promotional package for "Proverbs for Today" radio outreach especially for youth-oriented radio stations or programming. The package included radio spots on a small 45 rpm record, plus ads for youth groups to place in local periodicals. The "ad" shown here is probably the world's lousiest—and by an unnamed professional designer.*

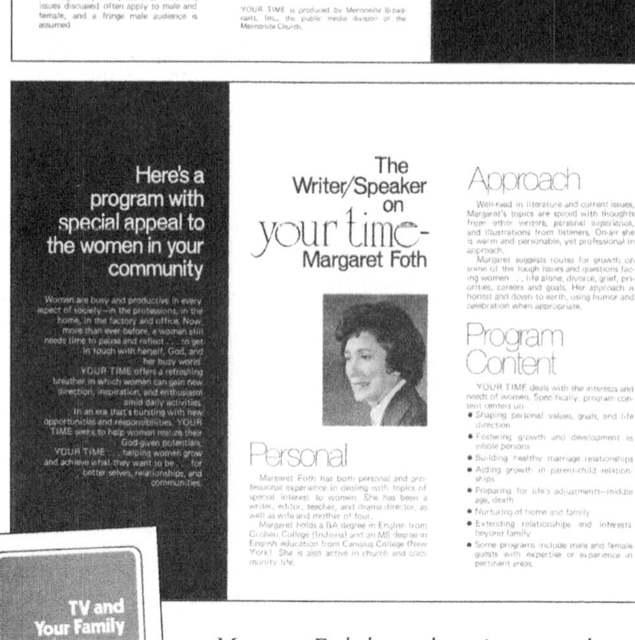


*Margaret Foth began her stint as speaker on* Your Time *radio program in 1977. Ron Byler joined the staff in 1979 and served as producer of various projects until 1993. Melodie did ghostwriting for Margaret once a month.*

CHAPTER 4

# When Mennonites Almost Took on Charles Stanley

When I joined the staff in the mid-70s, the heyday of that *Mennonite Hour* tour bus was about twenty years in the past. By 1975 we used only the previously recorded music library on reel-to-reel tapes. Our speakers, David Shank and then Willis Breckbill, worked from their homes and sent taped recordings and typewritten manuscripts to headquarters (no email, no thumb drives). We received a trickle of letters or comments from listeners each week.

However, anecdotally we heard there was still a faithful flock of listeners spending 15 minutes of their Sunday mornings listening to our flagship program. They sometimes did this while shaving or getting breakfast before church—most likely a Mennonite church at that. Thoughtful and earnest board members wondered, was this actual mission outreach—or discipling the faithful?

My workload included writing scripts for the opening and closing statements by an announcer for two 15-minute "teaching" programs, *The Mennonite Hour*, airing in the U.S. and Canada, and *Way to Life*, a missionary enterprise in the Caribbean region funded by several organizations. I unwrapped tapes for both programs, read through the scripts, listened to and timed them, wrote announcer scripts, and chose appropriate hymns to use before and after the sermon. There were more than 1,000 recorded hymns in our organization's musical archives by that time, making that part of my job enjoyable and spiritually rewarding. I did not listen to the recordings in my office (no access) but used hymnals to check the words and "fit" for each sermon or overall theme.

The final job as producer was attending an "audition" session (as mentioned in Chapter 1) where we simply listened through the program as engineer, producer, and one additional rotating staff person, who brought fresh ears to the program and the process. We listened for mistakes such as mispronounced words (rarely), do-overs that had been mistakenly left in, or most often, programs that ran over the prescribed length.

"Can you cut 15 seconds out for me?" Larry Heatwole, the exquisitely careful engineer I first worked with would ask. He knew my answer would be "Of course." Sometimes shaving off just 2 seconds was more difficult. As an organization we prided ourselves in maintaining the highest standards of production so as to never run too short (leaving mortifying seconds of dead airspace, a cardinal sin on radio), or too long, causing a DJ (disc jockey) to speed through his announcements or comments. Larry would manually pinpoint a section of the thin recording tape and move it back and forth across the parts of the machine that produced audible noise from the tape (sometimes sounding like animals in a barnyard: e-e-e-e-k-k-k-k), until he reached a break in the sound pattern, where he could splice out the extra-long space or material. He would then play it back to us to make sure the edit worked.

• • • • •

Before we dig into what eventually happened to *The Mennonite Hour*, first an aside on what happened in David Augsburger's journey with Mennonite broadcasting, and how it intersected with mine.

If you've never heard of David Augsburger, you are likely under 50 or have never heard of Mennonites. When I was growing up, Dave (his usual nickname) was a well-known Christian radio personality, almost like a Beth Moore or maybe James Dobson (not that Dave's thinking or viewpoints or writing were similar). Maybe Jim Wallis or Tom Sine or Tony Campolo were a more apropos comparison. He was probably the most prolific Mennonite/Anabaptist author for about forty years and Mennonite Broadcasts was lucky to have him in its fold for about twenty of those years.

Wikipedia says Dave is the author of approximately thirty books or pamphlets. Periodically we would ask him to come back and do shorter media projects called "Choice" radio spots. In the move to ever shorter radio programming, by the time I joined staff, the somewhat legendary Dave was on the west coast, teaching at Fuller Theological Seminary, and occasionally traveling back east to visit family (mostly based in Ohio and Virginia). He was game to continue serving as the voice on "Choice" radio packages, some of them revamped and repackaged from earlier runs.

I must add: The Augsburgers were a family of gifted and dedicated spiritual pastors, two others I knew pretty well. David's older brother Myron was president of Eastern Mennonite when I went to school there, and eventually Myron hired me to edit a book he wrote, *The Resurrection Life*. His younger brother Don was my pastor in Indiana and baptized me; my dad served as deacon under his leadership. Don was also my high school principal for a couple of years when I once got called to the principal's office for a reprimand (to my deep chagrin), but that's a different memoir.

I had heard Dave speak at several events as a teen or college student. However, there were times Dave fell on his face, or rather, "got skinned" as he put it.

The summer after I graduated from high school, I went to the Mennonite Youth Convention held at Lake Junaluska near Asheville, North Carolina (1970). David was a keynote speaker, along with Tom Skinner. But Skinner was absolutely on fire, full of good jokes and also deeply connected with that crowd on the topic of racism. I don't remember anything too specific either of them said, except for Augsburger, who later in the week, referencing Skinner's lightning rod speech, admitted he (David) "had been skinned by Skinner."

During my senior year of college, a carload of EMC students headed out to Goshen College (Indiana) where a Mennonite writers' conference was held. David was invited to speak and while I did not know him at all at that point, the students I hung out with sort of rolled their eyes about Augsburger's flashy bright red jacket. I believe in their minds, a red sports coat went more with a James Dobson or Pat Robertson kind of speaker. But please forgive the young creative college kids their snobbery—at least that is how I felt after I had the privilege to work with Augsburger a bit.

Back to the "Choice" radio spots that Dave pretty much "owned" and that were reworked into some of his bestselling books. In the late 80s, we started working on an eleventh set of "Choice" radio spots on the topic of "Facing Tough Times." By that time I had repurposed earlier "Choice" series for our production team, cutting 90- and 60-second spots down to 30 seconds to make public service announcements. But we wanted new original spots for the radio market. We brainstormed how we could use stories of struggle and difficult times from some of our other programming such as Margaret's *Your Time*, and another radio production of the day, *Passages*, by Dennis Benson (who died in 2021) and Presbyterian Media Mission. So as a writer/producer, I put the scripts together for Dave.

I had worked enough with Dave's style of writing and endings that when he came to town to record the new spots for "Choice" series 11, Dave said, "You know, as I read over these, it kind of felt weird."

"Oh?" I queried, scouring my brain wondering what he could possibly mean.

"The way you wrote them really sounds like me, my sentences, almost a 'parody' of me," he laughed.

I took that as a compliment, probably no higher praise for a ghostwriter. But I noticed that for the next series, circa 1990, he proposed writing his *own* spots. He suggested focusing on cross cultural communication in light of his recent experiences writing a book on *Conflict Mediation across Cultures* while living in southern California. He had done research in several countries amid the changing cultural landscape of the U.S. that some called "the browning of America." Dave noted in the spots that by the end of the millennium (1999), persons of other races and ethnic groups would outnumber whites in the U.S. for the first time since white Europeans started migrating over. We called the spots "God's Colorful World," which went on to be successfully aired on hundreds of stations.

• • • • •

The Sunday morning program, *The Mennonite Hour,* finally went off the air after 27 years at the end of 1978. Toward the end, a local popular pastor, Art McPhee, held the part-time *Mennonite Hour* radio gig for a few years. Board and staff felt it was time to end that flagship program with grace, but pondered how.

The board encouraged creating a new 2½-minute radio program for weekday drive times, appealing to a younger and more diverse audience, with Art continuing as the main writer/speaker. A recently graduated seminary student and eventual communications expert in his own right, Brian Lewis, was also hired as a researcher/writer for Art. The name we landed on was perfect—*In Touch*—for what Art hoped the program would do. Most of the 89 stations that were still carrying the longer *Mennonite Hour* went along with the switch to the shorter *In Touch.*

Then in 1982, we started hearing of a program by a little-known Baptist pastor, Charles Stanley in Atlanta. That program was dubbed *In Touch Ministries.* None of us felt that was close enough to our shorter *In Touch* to worry about. So we persisted with the program and the name.

One day, Lowell Hertzler, the adept business manager at the organization for over 40 years, stopped in at Art's office holding a letter. Lowell's face was somber and pale. "What do you know about the Charles Stanley program down in Atlanta?"

"Well, it's called *In Touch Ministries*," Art clarified quickly, "but I felt that it wasn't exactly the same as *In Touch*, when I proposed the name."

Lowell pushed the "cease and desist" letter across the desk so Art could read it. Lowell had received it from a lawyer in Atlanta. "They've copyrighted their program name *In Touch Ministries*, and say it is too close to ours," Lowell explained.

"But our program started before theirs!" protested Art.

"It matters who applies for the copyright first," Lowell pointed out. "We normally do copyright major program names, but it hasn't been on my front burner," Lowell said with chagrin. I doubt that any of the rest of us were pushing the issue, either.

Being good Mennonites, we wisely decided not to fight it. Membership in Mennonite churches in the U.S. and Canada is only a tiny fraction compared to millions of Southern Baptist adherents in tens of thousands of churches. For a small denomination, Mennonites had a much bigger media voice over the years than their numbers, owing in part to staff dedication and creativity, an eager and obliging board, and not to mention Mennonite more-with-less approaches (shall we say cheap?) to financing and fundraising.

As of this writing, the Charles Stanley program is still heard on numerous TV networks along with radio, puts out a regular magazine, and has a huge mailing list. Millions listen to Stanley every week and he's the author of 60 books, some of which hit the New York Times bestseller list. To Stanley's credit, he has avoided scandal and not flaunted any wealth in obvious ways as do some TV preachers. He was a "must view" for my 97-year-old mother every Saturday night for years. But for my kids who are mostly in their 30s, I doubt that any of them have ever heard of him, nor many in my own congregation.

In reality and church history, Mennonites and Baptists (including Southern) are close cousins in the Anabaptist stream of faith—both favor adults or at least teens making adult-type commitments to faith at the time of baptism rather than baptizing infants. Both Baptist and Mennonite predecessors were burned at the stake, drowned, and tortured for insisting on re-baptizing believers upon confession of faith during the years following the Reformation in Europe.

So, shall we say, it was a wise and Christian move not to fight these faith cousins. We obeyed the "cease and desist" order and changed the name of our own program slightly, to *Art McPhee In Touch*. Inwardly I hoped that our own denomination would not think that was being too commercial or haughty putting Art's own name in the program. Art's program ran until 1984 when the option to produce videos for church and broadcast began to come on the scene and we began to move into video products.

Would the organization ever get back to a daily radio program of its own? Was there still room on the air for a prophetic Christian voice for many issues of the day? If so, perhaps it would have to come at a later time, and a later director.

The threatening letter was not the only time we would receive such a letter in my tenure with the organization.

But there were plenty of successes. A brief paging through newsletters of the organization (*Media Connections* and later *Links@ MennoMedia*) leave me almost breathless with the variety of media we produced—which we'll get to later.

*"Choice" radio promotional packages, with voiceovers by David Augsburger.*

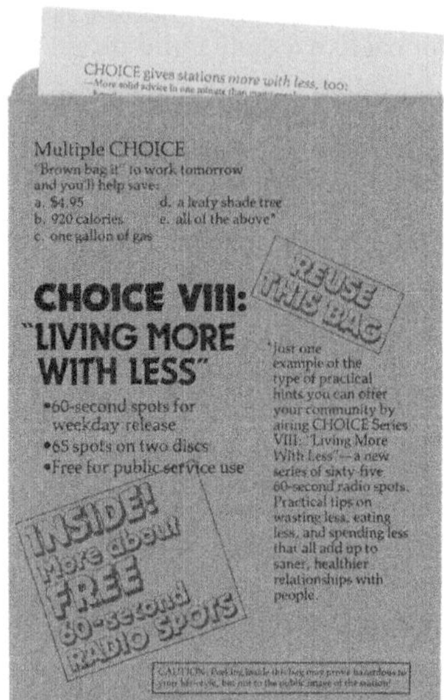

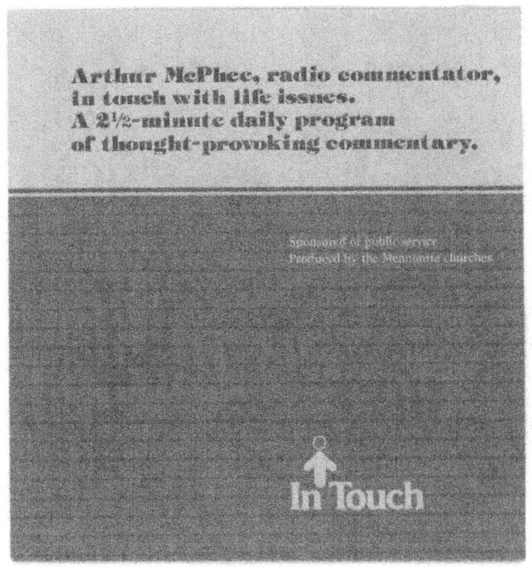

In Touch is a positive note in your listeners' day

- upbeat, stimulating content
- terse style that doesn't mince words
- humorous and heartwarming
- much more than just another devotional—just listen to the sample!

If you want a reputation for caring about your community, these day-brighteners with Arthur McPhee will help give your station credibility (and listeners!). *In Touch* stresses daily discipleship, authentic living, the centrality of Christ to all of life—but not in tired old clichés or tacked-on morals.

Commentator/Writers

*Arthur McPhee* is the commentator of *In Touch*. Past speaker on *The Mennonite Hour*, author, popular speaker and a pastor, Arthur brings wit and concise writing to the 2½-minute segments.

*Brian Lewis*, a seminary student and sociology graduate, teams with Arthur to research and write well-honed scripts.

On air, Arthur's approach is warm and personal, caring and direct. Listeners are invited to respond for free timely books or literature. Respondees are never put on a mailing list unless they indicate interest. Questions are answered by caring, thoughtful correspondents.

Program Particulars

Sample Program Themes

Do something for your audience you can be proud of!

Sample Script:

A daily "good news" commentary from Arthur McPhee and the Mennonite churches

*The* In Touch *radio program was launched with speaker Art McPhee and co-writer Brian Lewis in 1978, with the program name challenged (and changed) in 1982.*

*Longtime studio engineer Abe Rittenhouse, Ron Byler producer, and Melodie Davis as writer, pose with a Gabriel Award from the Catholic Media Association for "Choice," narrated by David Augsburger.*

CHAPTER 5

# The Diaper that Missed the Trash Can at O'Hare

"Five years." Did I say it as a jail term or an accomplishment? I remember the five-year mark of my employment at Mennonite Broadcasts because I wrote down some thoughts at the time. It just felt like a milestone worth pondering whether or not I was in the right place. For the most part I loved my job(s). But five years at *that* time, since I was young, still felt like a long time in one place.

Never would I have thought I could stick and grow with and remain excited about one place for so long. Five years is longer than high school. Longer than college. It was also about the length of time I spent at home with my mother full time before going to school. Not much time!

The five-year mark said to me that I had the maturity or whatever to stick at one thing and grow with it. I was happy I had a job requiring enough creativity that I felt fulfillment in routine work well done. In that, I knew I was very lucky. I was intrigued that perhaps my interpersonal skills had matured as well, to get along reasonably well with 26 others including part- and full-time folks. (Or perhaps they had the patience and goodwill to put up with me.)

A wider glimpse of our departments, mostly all in the same building at that time, included: program-related persons such as radio speakers, secretaries, correspondents and producers (seven);

Choice Books personnel (three to four); Home Bible Studies (two); Alive Recordings at a nearby converted chicken house (two); shipping and warehouse workers (two to three); accounting (two); news/fundraising (one); proofreading/copyediting (one); mail processing (one); marketing (two); plus company management (two).

Reflections turned to not just what I had earned in that amount of time—some $50,000 dollars, but what it meant to be working for a religious organization. I had to honestly wonder—was I *worth* fifty grand to the church in that time—from mostly donated dollars. Only God knew the answer to those questions but in my bones it felt good. In my heart I knew God was not so concerned about the fifty grand as whether I had served the Almighty to the best of my ability. Was I seeking God's will above all else? I felt the opportunity to work those five years in eventful, productive, creative labor was more than I could have asked or hoped for. These are the thoughts that many of us have as we look for God's guidance or when speculating on a new place of employment.

And I wasn't interested in even thinking about a different job. Occasionally I pondered whether I should consider getting an advanced degree—a master's. At seminary? In a graduate communications program? At the time, to pursue a degree in communications would have meant commuting fifty miles for classes to Charlottesville, Virginia. I didn't really want to drive 100 miles a day. But was I getting stale?

I also recalled my early major choice when I was beginning studies at Eastern Mennonite when I felt "called" to be a mission worker in a Spanish-speaking country, partly out of hearing faithful missionaries talk at my church all through my childhood. I also had the opportunity to begin studying Spanish in sixth grade (a little unusual in those days). Was I still listening for God's voice? After meeting and marrying my husband, Stuart, I began to realize I could be a witness right in our hometown of Harrisonburg. There were, and continue to be, urgent needs here. It is perhaps easier to discern calls to work or volunteer in far-off countries while ignoring the ways we can serve God "at home."

Mennonite Broadcasts slowly changed from mainly an organization doing radio programs and related follow up, along with marketing and fundraising—to producing a variety of media and formats. Along the way I kept my fingers in other projects, such as helping with a 15-minute Russian broadcast called *Voice of a Friend* aimed at people in the (then) Soviet Union. We worked with a native Russian speaker based in Belgium, Vassil Magal, to write and record the program. The vision was to help him also do shorter programming for newer audiences who may not have the inclination to listen to 15-minute programs.

Additionally, we related to a sister organization, JELAM (Junta Ejecutiva Latino-americana de Audiciones Menonitas), which was a Latin American Mennonite board producing a variety of mass communications in Central and South American countries. At times I was happy to be called upon to translate Spanish letters or documents.

But the overseas broadcast that affected me the most was *The Way to Life* radio program, which we produced for English-speaking populations in island or coastal Caribbean countries. We agreed to host a "trainee" in Mennonite Central Committee's trainee program who was from Jamaica. Trainees were typically between the ages of 18-25, so our first trainee was only a few years younger than me. I had the challenge and pleasure of mentoring Tony Young over six months as he learned the ropes of radio broadcasting for *The Way to Life* program sponsored by the Jamaican Mennonite churches.

Just recently I learned that Tony went on to be a successful and endearing radio host back home in Jamaica after his service term, but died from complications of diabetes the summer of 2019. A station colleague, Victor McFarlane said of Tony, "He remained ever fresh being 'Young.' He had worked at several radio stations and thrived wherever he was: Love FM, Roots FM and here at KLAS for so many years. He had an ability to work with just about anybody," as quoted in "The Gleaner" news website from Jamaica.

McFarlane spoke also to the fact that he considered Tony *his* mentor in radio. As I stared at the photo online of a man who at that point looked to be in his 60s, I thought, yes, that is the Tony I knew and worked with in his teens. The testament to his jovial spirit was certainly Tony. We worked with other "trainees" such as Norbert Funck from Germany, and over the years welcomed interns from all over who were looking for practical experience and training for their résumés. It wasn't always my favorite work, but it was a way to give back to those who had mentored me.

• • • • •

For my first five years at Mennonite Broadcasts, I did not know the pleasure (or stress) of mixing work or a career with raising a family. My husband Stuart and I got married almost one year after I first began at Mennonite Broadcasts, at which point I moved into the 45-foot trailer he owned in a trailer court. Our rental fee for that lot was $35 a month.

With barely enough room to even store all of our wedding gifts, we soon began not just dreaming of buying a house but actively looking. So two years after starting at MBI, we moved into a modest three-bedroom home about four miles from town. Perfect for a small family. I began pushing for us to think of starting that brood, and the conversations were frequent and sometimes heated. He knew I had tasted the heady wine of promotions and travel and feared I was not really ready to tie myself to hearth and family. "Plus, I don't really know if *I'm* ready to have a family," Stuart said at one point. "How can we afford it?"

"Well everyone feels that way I think," I argued in my round-about-way, "unless someone is really rich." As I sat silent and frustrated, I thought about how people formerly didn't have to agonize over whether or not to have children. You got married and then as sure as dirty dishes and income taxes, you had a baby. Or you at least tried. End of question.

"We managed to buy that little travel trailer," I reminded him.

"It was a bargain. And we both wanted it," he returned.

"We go out to eat all the time," I added.

"If you call McDonald's and Dairy Queen eating out," he shrugged. "And how will we ever afford everything we would need for a baby?"

"We spend money on your cat," I threw out in a mean streak.

Now he was quiet. That meant he was seriously thinking about it. Of course he wanted children, too, but knew he didn't make that much working in a factory.

Then, other young women I worked with began having babies, almost one after another. Six babies in the span of 15 months. We joked there was something in the water. Half of them left their jobs and the other three mothers returned to work, either full or part-time. The office climate seemed relatively open to women choosing either option. In our own situation, after about three years of no baby, we started to delve into whether we needed infertility treatments.

It was about this time when one of my close colleagues, Lois Hertzler, had a baby and she chose to return to work half time. I recall her saying if she had known how much she would enjoy having a half-time schedule, she would have changed to that a year earlier. She had been working 15 years (yes, right out of high school) and was one of the "always get it done" professionals who made us look good. I tried to cover for her while she was out on maternity leave, and learned how detailed her work was.

Her going to half time meant we had room in the budget to hire a new person, also half time. Ken recruited J. Ron Byler, who was recently out of college and had some experience in video work as well as overall communications. So, he was a real godsend at a time we were moving in new directions. Ron joined staff as a producer and to pad the marketing department. He was soon assigned to connect with organizations like the National Council of Churches Communications Commission (NCCCC). He worked for Mennonite Media part time for about 14 years while also pursuing filmmaking. Eventually he worked for Mennonite Church USA (1997-2010) in a key leadership position, and then was director of Mennonite Central Committee U.S. until 2020. I say all this because overall he was one of the most affirming and kind persons I was privileged to work with—always careful to compliment work well done and nudging me on to new accomplishments. A real encourager. We all need those.

Then boom. Yes, I was pregnant, too. Reality started to sink in. What would Ken say or think? How would I actually tell him or my colleagues? What if I got morning sickness—and worse, while at the office? MBI was super supportive of family life in its programming, but now that we were expecting, everything looked more dizzying. I told Ken first and I know his mind started calculating right away whether this would allow them to hire Ron full time. I told Ken I was definitely planning to return to work, but no more than half time. Maybe even just two days a week.

Three months or so into our pregnancy, I was invited to New York City for some of the NCC meetings. Before leaving on the car trip with Ron, I decided to pick up a pack of saltine crackers to take along in case my tummy started feeling queasy. I told my secretary, Evelyn Sauder, that I had to run to the grocery store to pick up some crackers before the trip because I was pregnant. Her eyes widened in surprise, but quickly swallowed that look. I doubt there was ever a more abrupt way to inform one's close colleague that you were pregnant than my awkward quick explanation to Evelyn.

On the trip, I told Ron that Stuart and I were expecting. He was not surprised and was appropriately excited for us. But as we tried to transverse the streets of New York City, I finally met Ron's nemesis in the form of city traffic. He got tense and testy driving those streets but we managed to navigate safely just the same. Out of the car, I breathed in the city air. Again, I reveled in the fact that my job allowed me to travel.

As a writer, I felt like going new places, meeting new people, and experiencing new things was invaluable for inspiration, and well, for my soul. It shriveled up when I was chained to my desk too long. After our family started growing, when invitations to meetings or conferences came my way, I looked for those which had childcare available, or meetings that were situated close enough to my parents in Indiana that they could babysit. I tried to find ways to take a child along with me on business as often as possible, taking turns according to their age, what babysitters or childcare options were available, and what we could afford in terms of their tickets or transportation.

Being able to take them along on adventures helped to make up for the things I missed in their early years by having to work part time. At least that's what I told myself when "working mother guilt" assuaged me. That doesn't mean travel was easy and I'm sure my boss sometimes wondered whether I could really juggle kids and business travel, too. I and one or several kids (after they were older) traveled together by train, charter bus, station wagon, minivan, taxi, and airplane. It was the early days of many mothers choosing or needing to work outside the home, and eventually I learned there was perhaps a price to be paid for that. I wrote an early "work memoir" about working and parenting published in hardback and paperback by Word Books, a big Christian publisher at the time. I was disappointed though when a major Choice Books distributor (Choice Books was headquartered in our office) declined to carry it on their racks because some conservative leaders did not think it was proper to promote women working outside of the home. (Remember I said in Chapter 2 this issue came back to bite me? And hurt book sales.)

One example here illustrates the challenges of combining work and motherhood. I had to travel through O'Hare Airport in Chicago before family bathrooms with generous changing tables were available. (And now in the 2020s, there are even nursing pods—totally private mini rooms where you can sit, rock your baby, and nurse. For a fee of course.)

My travel arrangements that trip included flying to Chicago, taking a bus service about 80 miles to South Bend, then having a sister pick up me and my two daughters to take us to Mom and Dad's. Mom and Dad loved the opportunity to babysit but now that I'm a grandma I know that babysitting sometimes brings panic (How will I get the kid to bed without Mom or Dad?) and frustration (Why won't they eat?) and Weariness (With a capital W).

I rode by car back to Chicago with colleagues from Mennonite Board of Missions in Elkhart for the meeting I was attending. And then did all this in reverse for our trip back home to Virginia.

As we were about to board the airplane at O'Hare, almost-four-year-old Michelle announced, "I've gotta go..." The bathroom seemed as if it was half a terminal away, and toddler Tanya was taking a much-needed nap. Luckily she was in the umbrella stroller, so I quickly grabbed the stroller, all our bags, perched Michelle on my hip and tried to hurry nonchalantly. In the bathroom, Tanya woke up and I quickly changed her diaper and asked the preschooler to deposit her sister's wrapped-up diaper in the trash can.

We scurried out because I thought I heard a boarding announcement. Out of the corner of my eye, I saw that the preschooler had missed the opening for the trash can and the diaper lay on the floor. What now? I didn't feel I had time to go back. Besides, my hands and arms were full: pushing the umbrella stroller, my huge diaper bag, purse—and a hand for the preschooler.

But then there was some delay and of course I forgot about the diaper that had missed the trash can until I overheard two female travelers talking loudly about the uncouth and thoughtless mother that "had not bothered to put her child's diaper in the trash can. She just left it lying on the floor. Gross!" I wanted to sink through the floor. It was probably one of my lowest moments in working-mother travels.

My scariest moment in traveling with little ones came the following year out in Ames, Iowa. The Mennonite Church convention the summer of 1985 was held at Iowa State University in the middle of vast cornfields. Literally. The cornfields backed right up to the edge of campus and made many of us Midwest-born-and-raised-Mennonite-corn-farmers feel so at home.

That year, I figured that my 27-month-old daughter (the one whose diaper ended up not being put in the trash can through no fault of her own) was the right age to go with me to the Mennonite convention. I knew she would have full-time nursery care available to her during meetings, and she was old enough to be reasonable about staying with complete strangers in a trusted setting. My older daughter, then almost 4 and a half years old, would be a great age to stay by herself with her grandpa and grandma on their farm in Indiana and help grandpa take care of his many piggies.

Before I left, I learned we were happily pregnant with our third child. I wasn't "showing" in the slightest, and morning sickness was slight if nonexistent. But I wasn't sharing the news yet either; we had decided to wait until three months along to announce it, just in case, you know.

So, the three of us, Michelle, Tanya, and I boarded a Mennonite youth bus from Virginia Conference bound for Iowa, leaving my dear husband all by himself at home. My parents would meet Michelle when it stopped at a Goshen College dorm to pick up more youth, and Tanya and I would go on to Iowa and return to Goshen after it was over and spend some time with my parents. The plan was that Stuart would then drive out to pick us all up in Indiana.

When Stuart dropped us off to board the youth bus, I recall him looking absolutely bereft: there we were, actually four of us (counting en utero), boarding a bus to leave him for two weeks. He couldn't have looked more mournful.

Grandpa and Grandma came to the college campus to pick up Michelle on time. Cell phones were not yet a thing. I have no idea how I communicated our arrival time. When we got there, Michelle walked off so bravely, carrying her suitcase packed with seven treats for seven days. She almost forgot to leave a kiss for me, and now it was my turn to feel like crying. Instead, it was Tanya who bawled, and I was glad she was going with me. (So was Grandma, I found out later.)

The rest of the trip went smoothly UNTIL everyone got off the bus at Iowa State in an area where they were depositing youth groups. Teens collected their baggage from the underbelly of the bus, and then headed off as youth groups or sponsors for their lodging, registration and a full week of activities.

Meanwhile, I was to find the "adult" area for dorm lodging and registration on a huge campus. The air started to smell like distant rain. Was that thunder I was hearing? Tanya began clinging to my side like a baby opossum. I tried perching her on one hip to collect my things including the bag with materials I had brought along to do presentations on "How to Hold Down a Job and Raise Children, Too."

I began to panic. Where was I supposed to go next and how was I going to get there all by myself? Why hadn't I done a better job of figuring it out in advance?

Another scary boom resounded across the wide Iowa cornfields. Lightning flashed and I tried to put up the umbrella we had been firmly instructed to bring. I stood there with daughter Tanya, depressingly out of hands *and* bravado. But suddenly, standing beside me, (I still am not sure where she came from), was Ann Yoder, wife of my co-worker Paul Yoder, director of Choice Books.

"Do you need a hand, Melodie?" she asked. Indeed. She was my guardian angel for that moment. We checked paperwork and discovered where the dorms were for me and Tanya. I think we boarded a campus bus or walked to that dorm. Somehow we managed.

The week turned out to be a special time of bonding with this, my second daughter, who was not used to having the undivided attention of mother. She called any telephone she saw a "Hello Daddy" and she looked forward to our chats as much as I did, even though I knew our phone bill would be terrible with me calling long distance. Grandma and I decided I should *not* call Michelle while gone, fearing that might provoke homesickness.

I made sure to take off from my convention duties one afternoon to go swimming with Tanya in the city pool, which we both enjoyed in humid Iowa. I remember thinking how her vocabulary advanced and matured right before my eyes—or was it only because I was usually too preoccupied to notice? She in turn cooperated wonderfully by taking at least one afternoon nap hiding neatly on the floor underneath the long tablecloth they put over every presenter's table in a seminar room.

And I was right, my oldest daughter had a glorious week playing with the piggies on Grandpa and Grandma's farm, not to mention the cat she loved dropping over the porch railing again and again. The cat did not seem to mind!

*Tony Young, an MCC trainee from Jamaica with the goal of working in Christian radio, confers with Melodie Davis on his next assignment.*

*By the time of this photo sometime in the late 80s, staff in the Harrisonburg office had been reduced to 20-something members. Front row: John Bomberger, Pam Shenk, Marian Bauman, June Lantz; second row: Lois Hertzler, Evelyn Sauder, Ken Weaver, Melodie Davis, Lois Priest, (short term employee) ______, Dorothy Hartman, Doris Sites; third row: Sheri Hartzler, Beth Benner, Patty Good Eckard, Renee Yoder, Jerry Holsopple, Carol Hamilton, Lowell Hertzler, Sue Pennington.*

*Getting ready to leave for work with two older daughters, Tanya (in arms) and Michelle carrying her favorite comfort pillow.*

CHAPTER 6

# Sex, Violence, and Videotape

Jerry Holsopple glanced around the assembly room at Mennonite Media. The year was 1989. Jerry was in the hot seat and probably nervous, but didn't show it. He was a recent seminary grad and energetic youth worker in central Kansas Mennonite churches in the 1980s. He had been asked to come to Virginia and bring his wife Mary, and their infant son Dirk for a family interview with staff.

Ken Weaver as director had already chased down a preliminary interview with Jerry off site, in his search to add youthful staff members to our fold. Ken's leadership was marked by an innate quest to stay current with the times and be able to speak to changing audiences.

As we introduced ourselves, Jerry pointed out their son was "named for Dirk Willems, the early Anabaptist martyr." (In the 1500s, Willems saved a captor who was chasing him across thin ice, and then was killed anyway for his faith.)

Ken grinned to hear Jerry's aside. He wanted this young Anabaptist maverick on his team and bad. He would dangle producing a possible new "video curriculum for youth groups" in front of Jerry to get him to move his family halfway across the country to the Shenandoah Valley.

Jerry leaned a bit on Ken, "Will you be able to find funds to gear up for a new avenue of work for Mennonite Media?" Video cameras did not come cheap, and in the early days of video production (before every Joe and Suzy could produce professional looking videos on home computers and smart phones), they would need to hire the services of at least a small production house to edit videotape—real tape, and a step newer than older film on reels.

When asked how he would go about planning content, Jerry spun out ideas like, "First we talk to this young teen…" and trailed off recreating in words the pictures he saw in his mind.

Ken wrapped up the staff interview and dismissed Jerry and family. The team left in the room salivated for this energetic young Anabaptist production-oriented mind that was already pushing edges. Would we perhaps remake the creative heyday of idea-hurlers like David Augsburger and Jim Fairfield?

A year or two later, a final video curriculum product with the title *Shalom Lifestyles: Whole People, Whole Earth* was packaged in a vinyl folder with slots to hold six videos and a leader's guide. Youth leaders could pop the videos into a video player for an instant, well-prepared (or at least well-produced) lesson. It was also a well-received product, and among the first video curriculum pieces produced by Mennonite Media.

Jerry could definitely deliver, but he rarely caved in to advice or input of others if he thought his was a better idea. Or unless he was squeezed. As a co-worker for ten years, I learned Jerry was super smart, creative, prophetic, willing to take risks, hard-working, and opinionated. I admired the heck out of him for his considerable gifts, and tried not to disagree with him. We knew when he came up with a dreamy design concept he saw in his head and wanted for the cover for a particular video project, not to fight him.

Many of our media projects, video and otherwise, went far beyond Sunday school and youth group audiences. In the mid-90s, Ken indicated we had money in the budget to maybe produce a public service announcement (PSA) for national television release. In the 70s, before I ever began working for Mennonite Broadcasts, there had been several successful flights of media campaigns the agency produced that included television spots in cooperation with other Mennonite groups. By the 90s, the Fairness Doctrine (yes, that had been a real thing) was no longer in play (abolished 1987). This "fairness" ruling of the Federal Communications Commission required television and radio stations across the U.S. to air public service messages because the "airwaves" were like the air we breathe, and thought of as universal property that should be used for the common good. Stations were required to keep records that showed they gave equal time in their programming for controversial topics or alternative viewpoints to what was commonly accepted as the status quo.

Stations were anxious for and receptive to such materials. At that point major faith groups, such as the Church of Latter-Day Saints, Catholics, Presbyterians, Methodists, Lutherans, and Mennonites all were in the public service production game for both radio and television.

Thus it was we were still producing radio and television PSAs in the 1990s, and together we brainstormed a campaign exploring alternatives to the violent responses we saw in many different parts of society. We planned TV and radio spots, print ads, and even transit ads for buses, subways, and billboards.

Jerry as video producer quickly weighed in on a topic that had been catching his attention. "Wouldn't it be *interesting*," (one of his favorite words when he was in the idea stage) "to show how we actually teach children that violence is ok and expected in certain scenarios, like on a ballfield? Why, just look at the parents!"

Ken encouraged him to go on. "Well it's no wonder kids learn to be disrespectful and even hit people sometimes—they often see such antics from their own parents when the kids play Little League games or basketball." Jerry soon worked up a storyboard for a spot showing guys—presumably angry fathers of players—shouting at a ref or coach, with small players running the bases.

With a go-ahead nod, Jerry researched and found a production firm who could organize the filming for the spot within budget. Jerry already had a lot of projects on his plate and he went with his gut, believing that to produce such a spot for television, the skills, equipment, and know-how of people producing commercials as a profession would also improve our game. That team came up with the idea of the ball teams wearing T-shirts that quickly showed the community nature of Little League sponsorship, with one team bearing the name "Lions" and the other "Rotary."

The TV spot opened with parents and spectators yelling angrily as a kid struck out. The kid then takes a swing at his helmet laying on the ground, and later we see the boy swinging a crow bar at a window. Finally, ending the thirty seconds on a positive note, we see a youth group working on building a house together. The spot encourages teaching kids kindness through service to others instead of violence.

The spot was filmed, finished, and sent to hundreds of television stations. We began seeing it on TV and hearing of others who had seen it. For a small agency and an extremely small budget (always doing more with less), it was heady to see or hear "Mennonite spots" on the airwaves.

And then a phone call came that was routed quickly to Ken as director of the agency. Rotary International in Chicago called to say they had heard from upset Rotary members about a television spot, which inferred that Rotary guys would cuss out refs at a Little League game. Furthermore, the spot communicated that this behavior could lead to violence in society—not a message with which they were anxious to be identified. And furthermore, there would be a lawsuit if our agency didn't immediately "cease and desist" from airing the spot. Lions Club International also wrote a letter indicating they had heard about the spot and were unhappy, too.

That kind of message pulls your shorts up quick and Ken, ever the Energizer bunny, scurried down the hall to confer with Jerry. He shut the door, always a sign that something momentous was afoot.

Later we learned that Jerry explained to Ken he had questioned the production company's idea for using the Rotary and Lions T-shirts (they were plain jane shirts, no logos used), but the production firm felt that it would not be an infringement on copyright since these were civic clubs and not saleable products as such.

Again we opted for nonviolence by immediately pulling the spot, and within days sent out "so sorry" letters to all the stations telling them not to use the spot anymore.

It would not be the last time we were threatened with lawsuits for trampling on toes.

Jerry was in charge of producing many other products geared more to church audiences. He produced *O Healing River*, a 38-minute video essay portraying basic beliefs and practices of Mennonites; *Many Grains* (similar theme); *Beyond the News* discussion videos (which also aired on cable TV outlets); and *Ted & Lee* (Mennonite comedy team) Bible story videos.

Jerry's vision for the *Beyond the News* series was to nudge Christians, especially, to deal honestly with issues confronting the church, which likely affected their ability to do outreach. He wanted people to feel discomfort with just maintaining the status quo. "If they don't get angry, they won't take action," Jerry posited. "While we want to be open to multiple viewpoints, we do not attempt to cover all sides of the issues. We are simply adding a voice to the dialogue in our society," Jerry said of the *Beyond the News* series.

The first in that line up was a somewhat daring video using actors to tell the true stories of persons who had been abused sexually. *Beyond the News: Sexual Abuse* was one of our bestsellers in this category of discussion videos from Mennonite Media. The video came out in 1993, about the same time as a Herald Press book was published, *Sexual Abuse in Christian Homes and Churches* by Carolyn Holderread Heggen, a psychotherapist. The books and video were something of a ground breaker in Protestant circles, and Heggen appeared in the video.

The stories that people shared in the video were gut-wrenching and eye opening, both for those who recorded the interviews, in post-production, and in the church—even changing how some viewed their daughters and sons or all children with whom they had contact. The video broke new ground. This was long before child protection policies were instituted by churches leading to windows on all doors of classrooms in churches, and always having two people leading a youth group or teaching Sunday school.

Another award-winning and disturbing video dealt with capital punishment and the racism that, historically, often affected cases. The program featured interviews with Bryan Stevenson in the early stage of his career in law and social justice, whom Jerry interviewed personally. (Stevenson wrote a book *Just Mercy* in 2015, and the story was made into a major motion picture released in 2019 starring Michael B. Jordan and Jamie Foxx.) In another edition, *Murder Close*

*Producer/videographer Jerry Holsopple (lower front right and in* Video Tip *photo on page 72) brought a burst of creativity in the 1980s and 1990s; Ken Weaver, Evelyn Sauder, Sheri Hartzler, Jerry Holsopple; second row: Lowell Hertzler, Wayne Gehman, Lois Priest, Erma Brunk, Lois Hertzler, Renee Yoder, Dorothy Hartman and Melodie Davis.*

*Up*, Jerry landed an interview with Sister Helen Prejean, the author of *Dead Man Walking* (which also inspired a movie of the same name starring Susan Sarandon and Sean Penn). Prejean of course wrote and spoke extensively on the depravity of the death penalty throughout the U.S.

Jerry seemed to have a sixth sense for whatever evil or societal injustice was welling up in the culture, and who was speaking out or acting to change things in meaningful ways. In that, Jerry continued a hallmark of Mennonite Media outreach efforts through the years. He invited us to journey even deeper into our faith and toward justice. He was frequently asking, "What does it mean to be a follower of Jesus in our times?" As an artist, he nudged us down new paths—some rabbit trails, yes, but isn't that the nature of creativity?

Violence was a frequent theme in our productions and outreach, both through the work and vision of producers like Jerry and Ron Byler, and executive directors like Ken and later Burton Buller.

And when events broke out suddenly such as the Persian Gulf War in August 1990, we put our heads together and brainstormed ways to produce and distribute an alternative message quickly to the press.

The Beyond the News *video series ran for several years in the 1990s on the difficult topics making headline news.*

**VIDEO TIP!**

*Jerry L. Holsopple, Video Producer*

**The Rule of Diagonal Inches**

*How large should the TV screen be so that everyone in the group can see? Use a screen that has the same or more inches from corner-to-corner as there are people in your group. For example, if your group has twenty people in it, don't use a TV smaller than 20 diagonal inches.*

## CHAPTER 7

# Bus Cards, Billboards, and Chicago's Oft-frequented Four Horsemen Hotel

In a small denomination like Mennonites, collaboration, interchange, and many broader meet-ups were a key part of the holy media moly, which Mennonite Broadcasts and Mennonite Media engaged in. The collaboration and broader meet-ups occurred over decades, so allow me to back up a bit.

Historian and prolific Mennonite writer John Sharp tells a quick "Mennonite meeting" story I loved in his author's preface to *My Calling to Fulfill: The Orie O. Miller Story*. In January of 1977, John was a recent college grad taking minutes at a meeting of the Mennonite Board of Education (MBE) at a motel near Chicago O'Hare Airport called the Four Horsemen Hotel. The hotel was popular with Mennonites because, yes, it had cheap (but clean) rooms and probably did not charge for meeting space. Like me, they probably assumed the hotel name was playing on the biblical book of Revelation's apocalyptic four horsemen. As my daughter pointed out—not a comforting reference for a hotel. A quick search online revealed the unusual name more likely came from a sportswriter for the *Chicago Tribune* who dubbed Notre Dame's football menacing backfield "the four horsemen."

That winter day, the meeting room at the Four Horsemen was abuzz that Orie Miller had died the day before. Newbie John was a little clueless.

"*Who is Orie Miller*?" John whispered to the person next to him. A longtime MBE staff member leaned over and filled in the young whippersnapper. The man they were talking about, if you're also a little clueless here, was one of the main persons behind the beginning of many Mennonite and inter-Mennonite organizations such as Mennonite Central Committee, Mennonite Economic Development Association, Mennonite Mutual Aid, and more. He literally saved many lives as Mennonites worked to bring food and relief to survivors in Europe after the end of World War II. Orie was also a much older, distant cousin of mine who grew up about 20 miles from where I did. Distant cousins are not hard to discover among ethnic Mennonites of the 50s.

So, willingness to write good minutes (such as for the *Heart to Heart* program speaker search mentioned in earlier chapters), and take on new or challenging projects such as the *Proverbs* radio spots I helped produce, eventually got me to that same Four Horsemen Hotel in the late 70s.

This was for a meeting of the Inter Mennonite Media Group (IMMG), which included Mennonite Brethren, General Conference Mennonites, Mennonite Church, and Mennonite Radio and TV in Canada—broader groups of Mennonites who cooperatively produced media reaching out to the wider world. I was thrilled to be in this larger circle, even with the humble assignment of jotting minutes (and no laptops). Those confabs broadened perspectives, made new contacts within the church and in the media, gave new inspiration to our organizations, and also functioned as in-service professional development. New graduates or those looking for a job change might want to keep these ideas in mind.

These meetings were often held in Chicago since it was central to many of the Mennonite agency players in the U.S. and also to

Kitchener, Ontario, and Winnipeg, Manitoba (homebases for those working in Mennonite media endeavors in Canada).

I felt a little awed. I was probably the youngest person in the room and one of two females at those meetings. I had heard both of my bosses, Ken Weaver and Dave Thompson sharing "Four Horsemen" stories at the office, which were plentiful in Mennonite leadership circles.

For the first meeting I attended there, we were brainstorming and working on a second multimedia campaign on behalf of the above-mentioned Mennonite denominations. The first had been in planning stages in 1974 shortly before I was hired. The new campaign was called "Invitation to Live" and it included everything from TV and radio spots, print ads, bus or subway "transit" cards, pins (for shirts), and stickers you could plaster wherever. The aim of the project was to counteract problems in society such as alienation, fear, and hopelessness. Keep in mind this was 1976, not 2020-21, but the issues sound like, as the writer of Ecclesiastes put it, "nothing new under the sun." The slogan capsulizing the campaign was "Invite someone to live by caring, sharing, listening, helping them to belong and become."

A later campaign that I did participate in more actively than taking minutes, was called "Reach Out: Be A Friend" and included a television special called *The Back Seat*, which first aired on KAKE-TV in Wichita, Kansas. It focused on the lonely people among us. One of the TV spots featured a young woman getting ready to board a Greyhound with an infant or two in tow. Another woman offered to help schlep her multiple bags up the steps and ended with the tagline for the campaign, "Reach out and be a friend." These aired on numerous local television stations because of federal rules requiring a specific number of public service announcements each quarter.

Our inter-Mennonite work grew the agency from denominationally-focused programming (*The Mennonite Hour*, *Heart to Heart*) to ever wider circles. Some would say we reached out too widely in participation with the National Council of Churches, which the

Mennonite Church never officially joined. But we took part in some of the communications committees who worked with the various networks on religious programming.

Another wider circle, an annual media gathering in Fort Lauderdale, Florida, birthed a consortium of interdenominational producers known as "Sandcastles International." I was not privileged to travel to Florida for those storied "beach" meetings. One year they landed on the idea that the most open opportunity for religious broadcasters may be the year-end holidays, Thanksgiving and Christmas. The producers who brainstormed the need for holiday specials reasoned that while advertising is rampant up until Christmas day, stations would be hungry for something to use on the holiday itself when station personnel preferred to be home with loved ones. The Sandcastles group also reasoned that the audience itself would be in a more receptive mood on Christmas.

I helped with scripting programs that included the likes of comedian/TV personality Steve Allen, and legendary Broadway theater, television, and movie actress, Helen Hayes. The programs' tags named all of the denominational participants including Presbyterian, Catholic, Lutheran, United Methodists, Mennonites, and Disciples of Christ with underwriting from the Protestant Radio and TV Center, and Church Women United.

Steve Allen narrated one of the vignettes I wrote. It was fictional, about a young woman who was scared to go home for Christmas because she was worried about sharing the news of her baby growing inside. It aired on stations plus the NPR network, and was broadcast in over half of the 50 major radio markets at the time. These programs were distributed to radio stations on 12-inch discs in a sleeve, like an old 33 rpm album.

The marketing department, along with the whole staff, was invigorated producing materials to promote these kinds of new programming, and diligently kept records on activities. As director, Ken saw to that, but he had the help of detail-oriented organizer, Lois Hertzler, whose name was on most of the marketing materials that went out to stations and church leaders. She would be the first to admit she was not a writer, but took materials that I or one of the staff working on a program drafted and then made lists of what went with each package, who would receive what, kept records of stations using our materials, and the like. She made sure that the rest of us met our deadlines and followed up if we didn't. When Lois came in to talk business, we perhaps spent too much time checking in on each other's personal lives, which I enjoyed. The camaraderie contributed largely to our staff knowing each other as people and not just co-workers. It can be hard to feel comfortable with that maybe as a boss, but as a team member she helped all of us work harder and become better organized.

Lois also worked with the design and printing cohorts on staff or subcontracted for various jobs with various persons filling that coordinator role through the years—most notably Evelyn McPhee and later Dorothy Hartman. We had a full-time excellent copyeditor/proofreader for the first years of my work, Mary Nell Rhodes who literally made sure all t's were crossed and i's dotted long before computers automatically flagged those slip-ups for you.

My everyday work during this time was ghostwriting for Margaret Foth and the *Your Time* program, as well as overseeing the production of *Art McPhee In Touch.* For Margaret, some of the themes and titles I wrote about included "Planning Your Will," "TV and Your Family," and "The Displaced Homemaker." The TV theme reflected my learnings from working as a Television Awareness Training leader. If you're not sure what a "displaced" homemaker is, it was a term in the 70s where women who experienced the death or divorce of a long-term spouse were suddenly at sea in how they would earn a living, back when the primary wage earner in most homes were men. (And certainly, caring for widows and orphans has long been a biblical directive for Christians.)

I appreciated the fact that even though I wrote this program content as a ghostwriter trying to reflect Margaret's perspective and station in life, in print Margaret was generous in crediting me as the writer. She was careful to fix any of my localized lingo that slipped through, writing a note to me on one occasion saying, "I see some colloquialisms slipping through from time to time."

We published printed leaflets of each week's theme, which we made available to listeners who subscribed to the print version, or wrote to request a copy of the radio broadcast. Her daughter Ellen, still in high school, provided the artwork for those printed leaflets and was identified as the illustrator. Margaret always sought to give credit to her helpers.

Margaret addressed the realities of the 70s—that women had more God-given roles than as babymakers and wives. Those were the years of the "total woman" mentality in some parts of evangelical Christianity. One Christian author, Marabel Morgan, wrote in one book that a wife could maybe surprise her husband at the door when he came home from work, wearing only baby doll pajamas. Maybe nothing is wrong with that, but Morgan's sexy ploy was more a way to get your own way in the relationship.

How do you measure impact? In reflecting on the effect of her eleven years with the program, Margaret said in later years, "In the long run, I think *Your Time* was influential in enlarging the vision of listeners to consider broader perspectives."

There was a cost to pushing edges, as Margaret—and all of us eventually found out. We were no longer producing sermons and hymns for the faithful to listen to as they got ready for church. Instead, we were attempting to catch persons in their daily routines and prompt them to think of the larger meaning of their lives and what they hoped to do for others and themselves. We were no longer patting women on the back and providing inspiration for staying home and doing the tough work of raising children—sometimes with little help from their spouses. Instead, we were encouraging women and men to be all that God meant for them to be.

The world was changing and Mennonite media programming

was constantly changing with the times. Perhaps we would have raised more money from supporters by sticking with old molds, but staff and board believed God was leading in directions that preached the power of love.

• • • • •

One of the longer running and perhaps most well-used media outreaches organized and produced by Mennonite Media was a yearly desk calendar that churches and pastors could purchase as year-end gifts for members, visitors, and outreach. The calendars also were used frequently by Mennonite-owned businesses as a gift for customers.

The calendars began in 1966 with 175 orders, the brainchild of staff member Eugene Souder, who helped launch more than his share of innovative media projects. The organization then began selling them to the tune of 18,000 calendars a year, which eventually grew to annual sales of about 40,000 calendars in 1977. The business manager for many years, Lowell Hertzler, shepherded the project through conception, development, printing and sales.

When I was assigned to be print producer, I also was asked to take on the yearly calendar project. We brainstormed and zeroed in on a theme for the upcoming year, soliciting photo submissions from photographers and photography agencies, and working with a team to narrow down the best for each year's run. In 1991, 340 churches ordered 55,000 copies; in 1996, sales dropped to 52,260 copies. The calendar project was transferred to Shalom Foundation in April 1998 (another media organization Souder began, which lasted until 2018). The calendars were an important part of Mennonite Media's outreach for 31 years. Users gave glowing compliments such as "People seem excited to receive such a colorful and attractive calendar" and "We appreciate its Christian theme." Another pronounced it as "positive, uplifting, and clear!"

But programming in a thriving agency frequently moves in new directions, and blessed are those who either keep up with the new adventures, or cut loose and make their own paths.[4]

*Melodie Davis and Mary Nell Rhodes, copyeditor, go over the calendar circa 1978.*

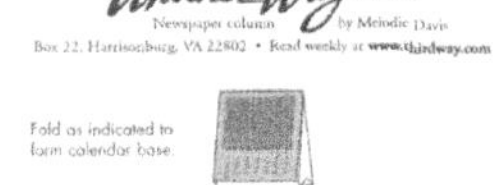


*Mennonite Media published and sold small desk calendars for income for 31 years, a favorite gift for businesses or pastors to give to their congregations at Christmas.*

---

4 (Margaret tells a very moving story from Orie Miller's life (the same man I mentioned at the beginning of this chapter) on YouTube as part of MCC's 100 years of service celebration in 2020. https://www.youtube.com/watch?v=bIdlyLj1aKY. After graduating from Goshen College, Margaret worked as head of the communications department of MCC for a two-year term.)

CHAPTER 8

# In the Days Before Churches Had Websites and Facebook

"It was just maddening! I was so determined I wouldn't..." my friend and colleague trailed off as she tried to recover from the news her program was being axed.

Everyone knows that of all the things you never do in a work setting as a woman, is let your boss or higher ups see you cry.

Most of us women would rather go through labor and delivery than break down crying in a meeting or with a boss. And it doesn't matter if the boss is also a woman.

At the same time, anyone who has ever worked for a church agency, a nonprofit, or maybe just been employed—period—you know the winds of change blow ill at times and budgets need to be cut. A board somewhere decides it has to gird up its loins and build reserves for the organization or business.

That is why I personally never aspired to be a CEO or executive director or even a departmental director, who was often the person delivering the "sorry about this" message.

• • • • •

Some broader history: In 1985, a church growth movement was percolating across Christian circles in North America, perhaps inspired if not challenged by other churches around the world who were growing faster than churches in Canada and the U.S.

If Mennonites were once the quiet in the land, pastors and leaders in the mid-80s "felt called to jerk the Mennonite Church out of its sluggish-growth doldrums" according to one *Gospel Herald* reporter at the time. It was at the Mennonite Church General Assembly in Ames, Iowa, in 1985—when I too was experiencing new growth (third baby in utero)—that delegates were inspired to take on the challenge of trying to grow 500 new congregations by 1995.

Mennonite Media director Ken Weaver sensed the value in jumping on board the denominational ten-year goals (later to be popularly known as Vision '95). Staff began brainstorming and strategizing how to produce new outreach media tools to help specific Mennonite churches be more invitational and introduce themselves to their communities. We'd long created "mass" media, since the early 50s. Now we sensed the wisdom of producing more personalized media.

In my one-on-one meetings with Ken, he broached the subject of putting my energies in new directions for the organization. Was I willing to spearhead creating eye-catching newspaper ads and direct mail pieces for congregations to use? Encourage churches to use telephone calls to help grow churches? I swallowed hard on that last one. Promoting telemarketing for churches did not excite me.

Ken always prepared even for a one-on-one meeting almost like it was a board meeting. He had an agenda, even if just a few scribbles on a yellow legal pad, a folder with my name on it, and a cleared table where he would share his latest dream or idea. He was one of those bosses that earned the nickname, Energizer Bunny. Always moving. Always percolating, in a good way. He would scuffle quickly into a meeting room and if he had not pre-arranged the set up, he would almost always move a chair or table or piece of furniture to his liking.

But a bigger issue at play at this time was the fact that our *Your Time* radio program was losing radio stations rather than gaining new ones. In the 80s, religious radio stations were, by and large, conservative evangelical rather than peacemaking pacifists or practitioners of nonviolence. There were also a lot of television and radio speakers who pushed a prosperity Gospel and who seemed to prosper and double their mailing lists. Those who didn't, sank in the ratings and lost the profitability of their airtime (local sponsors willing to pay for airtime). Many of our stations used the *Your Time* program as a public service for their listeners, but some arranged for local sponsors.

When the board decided to move in the direction of new shorter packaged programming, they didn't quite see Margaret fitting in that producer scenario. I recall Margaret herself reflecting she had become somewhat disillusioned by institutions, which frequently needed to do things by committee, which sometimes pleased the "lowest common denominator" on a specific action. She was so genuine in her relationships—always willing to do anything for anyone—and consequently assuming that others were the same way.

One week an executive from Mennonite Board of Missions, which had oversight for our programming, arrived in town for some meetings. One meeting was set up for Margaret, me, Ken, and producer Ron Byler for an undisclosed—to my memory—agenda. Presumably about the *Your Time* program. That's always scary when you don't know the agenda. Pre-meeting chatter as we gathered was nervous, stilted. I knew something was afoot, but didn't know how or when it would happen.

I don't remember precisely how the conversation went down, but it was painful to watch and hear, and extremely raw for Margaret to experience. She was mostly quiet, asked a few questions, and at some point, exasperatedly for her own psyche, bubbled into angry tears.

Margaret loved the program, the opportunity, the listeners, and the wide message she had shared in the ten plus years of the program's run. Margaret had steered the program into a more egalitarian framework for women and men in marriage and in the church. She recognized women were not just dutiful housewives supporting and nurturing husbands, but having dreams and ministry of their own.

The program also frequently addressed peace and justice issues. I had recently enjoyed helping Margaret move into an interview format for each program, wherein she had a guest each week participating in the programs. I got to help her gather interviews on cassette tape. The recurrent themes dealing with peace and justice spokespersons may have also moved additional stations to kick *Your Time* off their programming schedules. Fundraising efforts dwindled from the robust tens of thousands on mailing lists from earlier *Heart to Heart* days, to a small fraction. This was partly also the movement of the board to not solicit funds on air, and frowning on the souvenir giveaways of an earlier era.

When Margaret recovered her equanimity, she finished out the months until the program closed down with professionalism intact. In one planning meeting we looked at various aspects we needed to speak to—notifying stations, how to handle the fact that there would be less studio and shipping time and staff needed, and notifying listeners and those on mailing lists. It was a sad and disheartening time. Was it also the beginning of the end of ongoing involvement in radio programming, the bread and butter of what had founded the original Mennonite Broadcasts organization in the 50s? Time would tell.

At one point Margaret also graciously proposed a development that would affect the rest of my life. "I think Melodie should take over writing the *Your Time* newspaper column, under a different name of course," she said as my heart leaped with excitement. I had not considered that as a possibility, figuring the column would be kaput, too.

Several years earlier a fellow staff member, Paul Yoder who used to work for a "shopper" type paper in Ohio, suggested editing *Your Time* columns into a newspaper column as a way to grow Margaret's reach and audience. I edited each weekly column and worked with other staff and volunteers to sign up interested newspapers or church sponsors—some weekly papers and some daily. Margaret was happy for me to work on editing the column from her scripts, as she was always pressed for time to keep writing original programs and doing interviews.

Ken was game for this new column assignment for me and it seemed to fit logically under the umbrella title of "Print Producer." My own newspaper column? It was a little heady at first and several months later we came up with a new name for it, "Another Way," and a transition process for the newspapers. The column allowed me to have a "voice" in the media mix we produced—a regular print opinion piece and frequently spiritual in tone. I was very grateful.

Margaret herself went on to work for a conflict mediation center. Her interest in this area had been stirred directly from interviews she had done for the radio program. Later Margaret also served as community-relations coordinator for the widely-known Summer Peacebuilding Institute at Eastern Mennonite University. Margaret was also on the cutting edge of feminism and women's ministry in the church.

Over 30 years later in 2021, one woman touched by the program tracked down contact information for Margaret. She spoke with Margaret about earlier visiting the office because of the impact the radio program had on her life and spirit. Margaret was very much moved and rewarded. I don't think she's regretted her opportunity to spend over a decade creating a radio program heard by hundreds of thousands, perhaps more.

• • • • •

While the specific Mennonite Church denominational goals were not directly tied to closing out the *Your Time* program, I sensed that Ken had been pressured to pull the plug on the program. It seemed that overall, the physical distance of Mennonite Board of

Missions headquarters in miles (located in Elkhart, Indiana, while we were in Virginia), the frequent budget cuts, and Mennonite Media's methods of "mission" outreach did not help keep *Your Time* afloat. (Let me hasten to add I do not really know this, and memories and impressions can be fuzzy and erroneous.)

While church growth was a worthy goal also espoused by Jesus, "Go ye into all the world and preach the gospel," as the Mennonite denomination began to live with these goals, members peacefully argued over whether we should let numbers, or God, be our guide. One analyst noted that if the goals were achieved in ten years, the Mennonite Church would be the fastest-growing denomination in North America since World War II.

The "witness" objective itself was pretty astounding: "We pray that personal and congregational renewal in response to God's love and generosity, even through suffering, will lead by 1995 to:

- Doubling total witness efforts in existing congregations and in new cross-cultural urban settings.
- Adding more than 500 strong congregations of caring disciples—experiencing overall membership growth exceeding 50 percent in North America.
- Increasing the number of workers supported in mission beyond North America from about 500 to more than 1,000."

How did I survive that particular cutting back of program and personnel? I briefly considered whether I should resign partly in protest. I knew that would make things difficult for our own family—income wise—and also not knowing if it would be doable for me to find another job in the media field in our smalltown location. Move the family? We had just, a year earlier, birthed our final addition to the family—a third daughter.

Instead of quitting, I was asked to pivot to "print producer." One of the ideas on the table was to launch creative, professional products for churches to use in their local outreach. We had been producing a generic *What Mennonites Believe* type brochure, which took off from a leaflet that the ever-inventive David Augsburger developed in one of his radio sermons, "The Mennonite Dream." Some churches had privately produced brochures using all or parts of Augsburger's classic proposal, circa 1970:

> **We Believe...**
>
> That it is reasonable to follow Jesus Christ daily, radically, totally in life.
>
> That it is practical to obey the Sermon on the Mount, and the whole New Testament literally, honestly, sacrificially.
>
> That it is thinkable to practice the way of reconciling love in human conflicts and warfare, non-defensively and non-resistantly.
>
> That it is possible to confess Jesus as Lord above all nationalism, racism, or materialism. That it is feasible to build a communal church of brothers and sisters who are voluntary, disciplined, and mutually committed to each other in Christ.
>
> That life can be lived simply, following the Jesus-way in lifestyle, in possessions, in service.

Over the years, numerous versions of what came to be called "Mennonite Church brochure" were launched, and I was asked to spearhead its production. We also offered churches an opportunity to customize the inside brochure panels with their own church information: location, meeting times, staff, basic beliefs.

Thus we came to offer a production shop helping churches develop wording for church brochures—before the days of desktop publishing. Additionally, we produced newspaper ads, outreach cards (to be sent via direct mail to homes), plus radio and TV spots to help Mennonite churches get on board with Vision '95.

• • • • •

On the video side, Mennonite Media began producing what was called a "magazine format" television and video series we named *All God's People*. It featured Mennonite human interest stories, sometimes focusing on specific churches or individuals. We rolled out at least 18 episodes between 1985 and 1993 with Ron Byler as video producer, and later Jerry Holsopple picking up the reins.

I helped line up some of the initial families or individuals for the pilot program. "We are hoping you will say yes to participating in a video we're making showing others how God is at work through your congregation [or family, or organization]," I told them. People were usually surprised and flattered to participate, with some nervous worries about how they'd do.

Ron put them at ease by asking questions he was truly interested in hearing their responses to. Only one time did I hear about a participant who protested when Ron attempted to move ahead in the conversation about her husband who had died. "You got the book backwards," she reminded him. "I first want to tell you about who he *was*."

I enjoyed writing "host" copy to introduce the stories for our hosts, Duane and Nancy Sider, to be recorded. These programs were not originally intended for broadcast but rather to use in churches for small group or Sunday school class discussions, and included study guides with questions and suggested scriptures. Later on, some of the videos were used on the VISN Channel to which various faith groups contributed videos to reach a broader audience. A "Video

Club" was begun for churches to receive the *All God's People* videos automatically at a slightly cheaper club price.

We were also feeling a powerful need for a video that could compactly answer some of the questions that visitors to Mennonite churches often have. The idea had percolated in my mind for some time.

One day, if I'm remembering correctly, I kind of whipped out a script with some of the ideas I'd been mulling.

Ron Byler was my boss so I think I shared it first with him. He responded favorably and said, "Why don't we do that with animation?" I loved the idea, too, and was excited about exploring that medium.

We tested the concept further with Ken and other staff. Ron began looking for an animator. We ended up calling our somewhat whimsical video *Our Family Can Be Your Family*, which began with a guy walking down a street. He spies a horse pulling an Amish-type buggy and mutters (of course mispronouncing "Aye-mish… Menno-night?") until he finds someone who responds to his confusion. The fellow he meets answers his questions and gives a short history and key beliefs of Mennonites and Anabaptists. The video included snippets from the film *The Radicals,* which Ron helped produce earlier for the Sisters and Brothers film organization. Our video was the seedbed for a wider media campaign using the tagline "Our Family Can Be Your Family."

So the video, which launched at the Mennonite General Assembly in 1989 in Normal, Illinois, brought good natured parodies or take-offs from a group of young adults calling themselves Mennonots. I found their write-ups amusing and well-intended: Parlor Christianity: Our family plays Dutch Blitz better than your family; Below Par Christianity: Our family would really rather be your family; Insular Christianity: Our family can be your family, unless you're GC. (General Conference Mennonites were still a separate denomination.)

And speaking of family, I was able to take our youngest daughter Doreen to the Normal, Illinois, convention. She was old enough (three) to participate in the nursery and bunk in a dorm with mommy and one other roommate. Again we traveled by the youth bus from Virginia Mennonite Conference, but joined up with other colleagues from Mennonite Media who drove to Illinois for the meet up. We had a great week including an afternoon off from convention responsibilities visiting the city's pool.

• • • • •

Our work was ever changing, challenging, and fun because new or tweaked methods of doing and sharing media were constantly evolving.

Nevertheless, frequently as a new school year rolled around, I briefly weighed the possibility of continuing my education at the master's level. Should I look into taking classes at nearby Eastern Mennonite Seminary? Take classes across town at James Madison University or commute to Charlottesville for classes there?

But why? I was doing work I mostly loved and felt called to. Would people think I was not developing and growing as a person if I didn't have a master's degree or more?

• • • • •

"Do you really think them murderers should be forgiven?"

This question was posed to me in 1995, at the end of the Vision '95 decade while staffing our booth at the Mennonite Convention in Wichita, Kansas.

I looked up to find a man in a sleeveless shirt open to his navel standing in front of me. A tattoo decorated his left shoulder, and his gut looked like it had bellied a little too much beer. "Do you really think them murderers should be forgiven?" he shot at me again.

He was referring to the Media Ministries (the company name changed numerous times) video, *Beyond the News: Murder Close-up,* which looks at how families of murder victims have found healing through discovering the grace somewhere to forgive the worst. But what an opening question!

After I stammered for a response that wouldn't turn him away, he then quizzed me on Armageddon specifics and admitted he didn't have a religion, and that he had just come in off the street.

I invited him to take a brochure about basic Christian and Mennonite beliefs, which he folded three times and stuffed into his front shirt pocket already bulging with several other fliers.

He was relieved to learn that Mennonites did not believe in having more than one wife. I assured him that was a small sect of Mormons. I was relieved that he didn't seem to be just a man on the make. He had honest questions, and seemed like he was searching.

A future Mennonite or Christian? I prayed so. Would he be welcome at our churches? I prayed so. Are conventions worth it? This tiny incident did not prove anything, but multiply my few encounters by all the official and unofficial encounters other people had (amounting to thousands). I still pray that God will take all that went on in the various cities around the U.S. and Canada at conventions to change lives in ways that we never hear about.

• • • • •

Later in the day I watched a one year old toddling around the edge of the audience at the closing youth worship service in her nightgown. I thought back to when I had also toted my little ones along. No way did I envy the young parents at Wichita '95 their fatigue, but the fact that such assemblies are a place people want to bring their children is something to celebrate, and not lose.

I kept flashing back to the assemblies where my own children took turns attending with me: I brought one toddler to Ames, Iowa,

1985; another toddler to Normal, Illinois, 1989, when conventions were held on university campuses; and my 6th grader, Michelle, was able to share Philadelphia '93 with me. (Finally, according to her! She had been annoyed that she never got to go when her sisters had both done something before her, for a change. And by this time conventions were held at downtown convention centers with some fancy hotels.)

I thought back, too, to the last assembly I attended without any children, in 1977 at Estes Park, Colorado. That was in less-sophisticated Mennonite convention days. A small building there included just a few simple displays from Mennonite agencies, churches or causes. The Wichita Expo Hall, on the other hand, sported some of the most sophisticated exhibits yet—some felt too much so in light of Christian stewardship.

But, part of being church is running a business, where networking is extremely valuable. To meet, talk to, brainstorm ideas with, plan future work, and just hang out over ice cream may not at first glance seem like Kingdom work. But if Jesus were on earth today, I think He'd probably do conventions, like He did hillside teaching and healing in Galilee.

• • • • •

Speaking of business, some of the (now) cringeworthy items dutifully announced in our *Media Connections* newsletter that went to pastors, churches, organizations, and interested donors included:

> ...[January 1989] Installed a new toll-free 800 number for stations and congregations to use when inquiring about media resources
>
> ...[July 1989] You can [now] send documents to MBM Media Ministries in Harrisonburg and have it arrive the same day! We now have FAX equipment for quick receiving and transmittal of documents.

...[Also July 1989] Landstown Community Church in Virginia Beach, Virginia, used telemarketing to invite people to church. Volunteers dialed 16,000 phone numbers over four weeks. They spoke to approximately 11,000 homes and for those who did not have a church home, the volunteers asked permission to send mailings inviting them to their new sanctuary.

*A series of* All God's People *videos featuring mostly Mennonite churches, groups, and stories (with study guides to aid group discussion) were produced by Jerry Holsopple and Ron Byler.*

Our Family Can Be Your Family *video, produced by Ron Byler, also launched a group of print media resources for churches to use in reaching out to newcomers in their communities.*

CHAPTER 9

# The Backward Horse and How We Got There

For a long time, I loved collecting some of the early misspellings of *Mennonite Hour* such as Midianite Hour, Man of the Knight Hour, Minnow Nite Hour and more. If you've never heard of Mennonites, and you hear Men-o-nite on the radio, the spellings can get fun.

But this touches on one of the pervasive issues regarding Mennonite Media sharing the good news with the secular public: a basic confusion about who Mennonites are, or differences between Mennonites and Amish. This was especially important before the changes wrought by the World Wide Web and instant information. Now most people are able to instantly Google or ask Alexa a question like "What is the difference between Mennonites and Amish?" and get a plethora of results.

So, as the Mennonite Church worked at growth especially during the Vision '95 decade, an advisory committee for Mennonite Media was organized in 1989. The committee included several Mennonite Board of Missions staff people, three pastors, and four media professionals. My boss Ken thrived on making sure we were connecting with denominational priorities and goals, and not running his own ship. Thus, my own work as a producer took on various forms with our team, including research, brainstorming, testing, revising and launching—no time to get bored! And, opening ourselves to occasional blunders.

• • • • •

If you ask a random person on the street what they think of when they hear the name Mennonite, two out of ten persons will not know what to say, probably even today. (That depends of course on the area in which you live.) Or, the response will have something to do with Amish, Mormon, or maybe even Moonies.

Spurred on by this confusion, Ken as director of Mennonite Media worked with the Mennonite Church to conduct professional research in 1988-89. The research basically revealed that about 36 percent of the 1,200 persons surveyed by telephone said they know nothing at all about Mennonites. Almost an additional 40 percent of the persons knew only the name, or indicated understandings of Mennonites limited mainly to horses, buggies, black dresses, and black hats. In total, over 77 percent of those surveyed had wrong or very limited understandings of Mennonites. This was in comparison to four other churches or denominations from small to large size, which were Catholic, Baptist, Lutheran, and Mormon. Two-thirds were aware of the Mennonite Church as compared to a 94 to 98 percent awareness level for the other churches.

You might think confusion about Mennonites is better than scoring a zero when asking people about their awareness. It is difficult to undo an image; it may be more difficult to undo an image than not *leaving* an impression.

Images and references to Amish popped up from time to time and I began to pay attention to derogatory jokes about Amish on primetime TV. Here are a few examples on TV from 1994:

> On *Boy Meets World*, the husband was trying to cajole his wife, who was wearing plain flannel pajamas, into bed. He tells her the pajamas look *"positively Amish!"*
>
> On *Love and War*—the show that came on for a while after *Murphy Brown*—a man was talking to his girlfriend about the fact that she doesn't watch much

TV. She says, "I don't like TV, I don't even own a TV."
He countered, *"What are you, Amish?"*

From pop culture, on radio, there was Weird Al Yankovic's parody of "Gangsta's Paradise," dubbed "Amish Paradise," approximately 1996.

These can be considered put-downs for the Amish, not Mennonites. But since there is so much blurring in the public mind of Amish and Mennonites, this type of reference was cause for a bit of concern for us at Mennonite Media working at building positive images. As far as I know there is no PR department for the Amish, nor do TV writers generally have to worry about the Amish seeing/hearing these jabs. Years later a few producers and youthful Amish on *rumspringa* participated in reality TV shows that left additional images and information in the public mind.

A little history here might be helpful. Mennonites and other Plain groups are of course from the same stream of faith, most tracing their roots to the Anabaptist movement within the Reformation in Europe, and are proud of this common heritage. However, many—but not all—feel that some newcomers are put off by the feeling that "Mennonites are too different and I cannot be one of them."

Most Mennonites do not distance themselves from Amish because of smugness or distaste, but to offer a more welcoming stance for those interested in becoming part of their church. In recent years, there has been a significant move for numerous Mennonite churches to take the "Mennonite" out of their name.

In another research effort, in 1994 I helped lead a partnership with Mennonite Central Committee (MCC) to hire a "clipping" service to send us actual newspaper and magazine clippings using the words "Mennonite" or "Amish." (I know: No one needs a "clipping service" today when you have Google.) MCC was interested because of all the Mennonite-related organizations or agencies, they got the most "press" unless it was also Mennonite Disaster Service. Both of these groups frequently show up when there are disasters and work to provide aid and recovery.

The clipping bureau combed approximately 17,000 periodicals during this time for any mention of the word Mennonite. They eliminated an extensive list of Mennonite-related periodicals, weddings, obituaries, and birth announcements (or as one of our church editors dubbed them, the "matched, snatched, and hatched" columns). The clipping bureau also eliminated church listings and advertisements. The result was a delightful, amusing, and sometimes maddening diversity of stories.

What we found was a healthy, and sometimes amusing *variety* of images: buggies, capes, earrings, cow manure sculptures, a woman who helps run a contracting business, relief sales, and four shirtless "hunks." All these images had the word "Mennonite" attached to them in some way in the nation's (U.S. only) press from September 15 to December 15, 1994.

The good news is that the images were slightly more positive and the writers more informed than we expected. The high number of positive mentions may be in part attributed to many articles regarding MCC relief sales (large community fund-raising events) and self-help craft stores during the key "relief sale season."

The clipping service covered periodicals ranging from very small newspapers with free circulation, to large, slick, national and international magazines. The *Los Angeles Times*, *Baltimore Sun*, *Pittsburgh Post-Gazette, Orlando Sentinel, Columbus Dispatch*, *Philadelphia Inquirer*, *Washington Post*, *Houston Post*, *Miami Herald*, and *Atlanta Constitution* all ran articles about Mennonites.

A co-worker, Shirley Nafziger (later Brunk) catalogued clips under my direction. This was admittedly a subjective process—a different cataloguer might have interpreted the mentions as positive or negative. The project did not provide any measurement of how people were actually impacted by these images and stories; we also did not do post studies regarding impressions and awareness of Mennonites. It stood as a sampling of what the coverage looked like during that time period.

One very interesting mention concerned a group calling themselves "606," a rock group in Sarasota, Florida. It was making waves on the club scene there at the time. They also still apparently kept one foot in their religious beliefs, reported the magazine. "606" was a hymn number in an older hymnal for an arrangement of "Praise God from Whom All Blessings Flow." The anthem is so well-loved and exuberantly sung at large Mennonite gatherings that it has also been called "The Mennonite Anthem."

Jurg Rindlisbacher, a Mennonite journalist from Switzerland who helped us look at the data, noted that rather than trying to spend a lot of energy defending or correcting portrayals of Mennonites, "Fill the media with positive stories and correct images so that it becomes common knowledge that there are many kinds of Mennonites and Amish."

Still, the stereotypes have made it difficult to welcome people to the Mennonite brand of being "church" as noted in these anecdotes from my files:

- A Mennonite pastor was cashing a church check with the word Mennonite on it. The teller noticed it and remarked that she often had a very strong desire to stop in for a service at a Mennonite church she drove by frequently. She was curious about what Mennonites did in church on Sunday morning. But she was afraid to take the risk, not sure if she would be welcome.
- A Christian bookstore clerk in Springfield, Ohio, told the Mennonite Publishing House that sales are frequently lost when a non-Mennonite customer finds out that a particular book they have shown

interest in is published by a Mennonite publishing house.

- Our office received a letter from an Episcopal woman who was wanting to explore more about the Mennonite Church. "I've talked with my family and friends and they all say, 'No, you're not able to do anything [in that church].' Everyone I've talked to says it is not a good idea for me to get involved with the Mennonite Church."

As a result of this varied research, both professional and anecdotal, Mennonite Media launched an extensive media image campaign dubbed "Mennonite Identity Media" that included TV, radio, and print ads, some of which are displayed on page 104. We used the "Our Family Can Be Your Family" theme and slogan from the 1989 video to earmark most of the campaign.

One of the creative persons who wrote scripts for the *Art McPhee In Touch* radio program, Brian Lewis, had grown his own ad agency by this time. He was adept at arranging photography, headlines, and wording to create thought-provoking ads that would compete in the marketplace. Someone proposed that we contract with Brian to produce professional print ads that could be used by congregations.

Thus several of us loaded up a staff car and drove two hours to Richmond, Virginia, to meet with Lewis at his ad agency. The office there made me feel almost like I was entering Madison Avenue—so modern and citified. Lewis was not a Mennonite but had met numerous Mennonites at Fuller Theological Seminary, and was somewhat acquainted with both the good and beautiful parts of being Mennonite, and the bad, the ugly, and misconceptions. He was able to write ads that were fetching and sometimes humorous at the same time, such as:

For Anyone Who's Ever
Wondered What Mennonites
Are Like, We Have A One-Word Answer For You.
WELCOME

If you've ever thought the Mennonite church was some kind of closed fellowship, we'd like to set the record straight. We'd like you to know that you're wanted. And needed. In the Mennonite Church. You know us as the Mennonites, but do you really know us? This Sunday, take a face-to-face look.

The Mennonite Churches: Our Family Can Be Your Family.

The ads contained a small inset photo of a variety of real Mennonites, and a place for the local congregation to plug in their name, address, or phone. (No one was using websites at this point.) Incidentally, later in the decade from 2010-20, some pastors embraced this "WELCOME" message as the church became increasingly open to all people—and loved the poster size.

Another ad that became popular in poster size with Mennonite tourist information centers showed a horse tied to an Amish buggy backwards, with the headline:

Ask Some Mennonites To Hitch
Up A Horse and Buggy, And You'll
Either Have A Confused Horse,
Or A Very Strange Ride.

If you think all Mennonites look, think, and live the same, you better think again. Ask this poor horse what we mean. He'll tell you all Mennonites aren't alike.

> You know us as the Mennonites, but do you really know us?
>
> This Sunday take a face-to-face look at a church that may surprise you.

In addition to newspaper ads, Jerry Holsopple worked with Baltimore Film Factory in Baltimore, Maryland, to produce two TV spots with the general message that anyone is welcome in the Mennonite Church, and citing key beliefs. Staff also produced radio spots through our inhouse Alive Recordings studio and used the same themes as the print and TV ads.

The Johnstown, Pennsylvania, area has long been home to numerous Mennonite churches, and the churches there climbed on board the Vision '95 effort to enlarge and reenergize the existing congregations. Staff members Jerry Holsopple, Ron Byler, and Ken Weaver connected with pastors there to work on a coordinated outreach media effort. They used billboards, newspaper ads, radio and television spots, direct mail and telephone. They worked with a local radio station to produce spots specifically for their area. Surveys conducted before and after the media campaign revealed one statistically significant change—a 72 percent increase in the number of Johnstown residents who could name a local Mennonite church.

"The pastors agreed that media exposure alone was not enough to bring visitors into their churches," reported pastor Kurt Horst. "But it was also clear that the media campaign had a wonderful positive effect on the congregations themselves. They are taking themselves seriously, shown by more members becoming more active in their churches, and young people more ready to invest energy in their congregations." [Quotes from *Media Connections* newsletter, August 1990.]

Overall, the good news is that the image campaign seems to have had some effect, or perhaps we should credit news people with doing a better job of *getting* the difference between Mennonites and Amish.

In a *Newsweek* "My Turn" column in 1993, a young Jewish student, Chana Schoenberger, noted that even the smartest students were amazingly ignorant about religious differences. She relayed a conversation from a group of students in an honors program with a diversity of students including Jewish, Catholic, Muslim, Hindu, and others. On the first day, one girl mentioned that she had nine brothers and sisters. "Oh, are you Mormon?" asked one girl, who was Mormon herself. The first girl, shocked, replied, "No, I dress normal!" Schoenberger said that the girl mistakenly thought Mormon was the same as Mennonite, and the only thing she appeared to know about either group was that Mennonites dress weirdly. Schoenberger, as a Jew, added that she has been asked if she practices animal sacrifices. (*Newsweek*, Sept. 20, 1993, p. 8.)

So it is certainly not only Mennonites who struggle with misconceptions and old images. I have not even alluded to the current struggle regarding some misconceptions of Christians as right wing wackos. These days, a priority might be encouraging persons with faith, intelligence and a good sense of humor—to do a better job of filling the media with *alternate* images and stories regarding people of faith.

The success of the "Our Family" campaign, which helped the public better identify Mennonite people, churches, and faith, compelled staff to again work with Lewis Communications for a new campaign.

Three new outreach ads—one called "Faith at Work" came out in November of 1990. They were designed to be a companion series to the "Mennonite Myth" ads. The new ads placed an emphasis on service as a hallmark of Mennonites.

And perhaps we overreached at times. As we'll discover in the next chapter.

Mennonite
Board of Missions

CAMERA-READY ADS

This ad is camera-ready for use in newspaper, yellow-page and other similar media. The ad may be enlarged up to 20%. More than a slight reduction of the ad should be avoided.

For Anyone Who's Ever Wondered What Mennonites Are Like, We Have A One-Word Answer For You.

If you've ever thought the Mennonite church was some kind of closed fellowship, we'd like to set the record straight. We'd like you to know that you are wanted. And needed. In the Mennonite church.

The Mennonite church is open to all. To be a Mennonite you just have to be committed to Jesus Christ and His people. It's as simple, as hard, and as complicated as that.

You know us as the Mennonites, but do you really know us?

THE MENNONITE CHURCHES.
OUR FAMILY CAN BE YOUR FAMILY.

Congregation name and i.d.

*"Welcome" ad conceived and designed by Brian Lewis, who earlier assisted Art McPhee in script writing.*

*Sparked by various ads offered by Mennonite Media, Johnstown (Pennsylvania) Mennonite Church teamed up with a billboard company to run a series of ads inviting people to join their "family."*

CHAPTER 10

# Muscular Mennos: *Newsweek* and Beyond

Who would imagine that a church-based advertising and media outreach, from a denomination that was considered modest, simple, and conservative in lifestyle, would ever be accused of capitalizing on "beefcake"?

I think the idea to go big with a print ad was most likely our director Ken, because he certainly was the gatekeeper on finding squirrelly line items in the budget that could help pay for such an experiment.

In our efforts to create advertising more directly cued to introducing newcomers to Mennonites and Mennonite churches, we toyed with the idea of a major print advertisement in a large, widespread, and respectable magazine like *Newsweek*. It was one of three popular news magazines of the time.

The "Mennonite Identity" effort—with radio and TV spots and a flurry of newspaper ads usable by local congregations on the "Welcome" theme, was already well underway for a couple years when we decided on a full-page ad for *Newsweek*.

I wish I knew for sure who had the original idea. Sometimes good things do arise out of a committee. Someone says something and the next somebody adds on and before you know it you are rolling. That's in the best committee times, and we had some.

I do recall we all quickly jumped on board. Ken said we could spend up to $20,000 or so on a major ad purchase. Ken or Allen Angell, our marketing associate who joined the staff in mid 1991, negotiated a "religious" or "nonprofit" discount with *Newsweek*. We narrowed the ad buy to the six states that had the most Mennonite churches: Illinois, Indiana, Maryland, Ohio, Pennsylvania and Virginia. Thus we ended up with enough budget for two separate ads, about three months apart. The original retail value of one ad in *Newsweek* covering six states was in the neighborhood of $23,000, but with a 4 percent nonprofit discount, our 15 percent agency discount commission, and a 2 percent discount for paying cash, we ended up paying $11,341. Like good frugal Mennonites.

The thought was that it would be best to advertise in states where there were actual Mennonite churches nearby (no Nevada or Utah locations). We knew from our work in answering emails, letters, and phone calls that people were sometimes understandably upset and frustrated in trying to find a Mennonite church in their area. Especially when they had an affinity for things Mennonites stood for, such as nonviolence and service to others. Thus they were frequently disappointed to find out there was no Mennonite church within 100 miles of their location. No websites to quickly check, either.

Brian Lewis can be properly credited as the guy who came up with our two ads, the first one a heart-hitting photo of a man working at a desk in an office late at night with the slightly judge-y message "Working Late Again?"

We carefully designed and tested several mock ads, including at several airports and at least one shopping mall, to get opinions on which of the two sample ads should be used in *Newsweek* on the family theme.

Ken, Allen, his assistant Dee Stutzman, and I interviewed shoppers at a mall in Richmond, Virginia. Most shoppers were happy to comply, and were pleasantly surprised when we handed them a dollar bill at the end of the short interview, to thank them for their time.

Having planned to get opinions from only 15-20 people, we

hadn't thought about needing to get permission to conduct the surveys. So when one security guard came up to us, we asked her if she would participate in our market research. She said we weren't allowed to do that in the mall, and asked us to leave.

But as she disappeared, we approached another shopper, just to get another opinion. Suddenly there were two security guards coming toward us. "We will remove you from the mall if you don't leave," was the message one conveyed in a stern (menacing?) voice. At that point we quickly and respectfully left, thoroughly embarrassed.

I felt like a student called to the principal's office. Did that security guard look upon us with the same kind of pity and scorn I directed toward some street preachers—or the children distributing tracts to fans streaming into a college football game?

The feedback we had managed to get was helpful. Combined with research gathered at four airports over several days (where none of us were kicked out!), we had good feedback on which ad connected best.

This new ad showed a lonely man in a dimly lit office hunched over his work well after closing hours. His hand propped his head, implying he was working late. Again. Even though you don't see a family, the ad encouraged readers to balance work with time for family and friends. It ran in *Newsweek* in February 1993.

But perhaps the most important thing we learned: Get permission before you do any "market research" or any kind of "outreach" at a mall. Or football stadium, I'm sure.

Smaller ads were made available to Mennonite churches to use locally. I don't recall any negative feedback and numerous churches used them. And in our newsletter, we shared the overwhelming news that "You really should get permission to do any canvasing or research at the local mall."

• • • • •

The second ad ran in a late May 1993 issue of *Newsweek*, planned to appear a week before the Mennonite General Assembly (convention) meeting in Philadelphia, Pennsylvania. The first mock-up of the ad showed a young man in his teens or early twenties working with bib overalls (shirtless) on the roof of a house. It presumably depicted a realistic scene like Mennonites volunteering for disaster relief projects such as those run by Mennonite Disaster Service. The message for the ad included this:

**Muscular Christianity**

> In the Mennonite Church some of our most satisfying work-outs take place not in gyms but in the yards of hurricane victims and the homes of the poor. Satisfaction happens when you put Christian faith into action by choosing a life of giving, instead of a life of merely getting. This Sunday, check out a church that will challenge you to sweat . . . to work out your faith in ways that make a difference.

Somehow the final photography for that ad morphed into *not* a slim young Mennonite-looking man in bib overalls, but a super hot and beefy shirtless guy, who perhaps had a bit too much greasy shine on his chest, perfect hair, and bulging biceps. Critics complained it was "beefcake" and asked whether we would have ever used a female that way. Others who were more positive—complimented the ad's verve and power to capture attention and explain who Mennonites are and what they believe.

The ad definitely got conversations going. As they say in the advertising world, perhaps wrongly, there is no such thing as a negative ad. If an ad provokes controversy and conversation, that leads to word-of-mouth exposure, which is always the best advertisement.

So, one day at the office I got a phone call from a young woman from of one of our national Mennonite periodicals. She was the news editor digging for more information on the *Newsweek* experiment, and wanted to know what we had paid to run it. I knew the wisdom of spending donated money to purchase space in a magazine like *Newsweek* was maybe questionable for some people, and while I can't remember whether we as staff discussed whether the amount would be disclosed, I ducked. I said I was just the producer and not at liberty to share the cost, in my nicest dodgy voice.

She did not push and I thought, whew, evaded that one.

I found out later she went higher up and got the information straight from the ad sales people at *Newsweek*, inquiring for the cheapest non-profit rate for an ad in six states. When the cost came out in print in the *Gospel Herald* (changed to *The Mennonite* in 1998) I was pop-eyed. What? How? Yeah, she was an investigative journalist in this case and felt called to do a little digging when she had to, something I never really aspired to do. I've long since forgiven her of course in my mind.

The Muscular Christianity ad was seen and shared in many places (long before there was Facebook or the Internet) and went on to be used in at least one textbook by a communications professor writing a book on media. An additional irony (was it intentional by *Newsweek*?): That particular *Newsweek* issue ended up with a genuine Amish man on the cover, fighting through the muddy waters of a flood.

Eventually Levi Miller, an editor at Mennonite Publishing House at the time, wrote a news release printed in *Mennonite Weekly Review* revealing the name of the Amish guy on that cover, Solomon Schwartz of Missouri, age 26. Levi himself grew up Amish. David Luthy, a publisher of Old Order Mennonite materials in Ontario who I later worked with in the years I was an editor myself for the Herald Press division (see Chapter 15), noted that Schwartz was most likely a baptized Amish church member but unmarried.

"How did he know that?" Levi queried of Luthy, because various groups have differing customs.

"His short beard indicates that," responded Luthy, back to Miller.

I wonder if some worldly-wise young Amish woman may have worked to change the unmarried status of the guy on front of *Newsweek*, the real-life Anabaptist-stream muscle man.

The ad was parodied (certainly a form of flattery) on an old and early website, Mennonot, which at one point was a humor paper. I think I can credit Cole Arendt with writing this:

> "What follows is other ideas for how Mennonite Christianity might be sold to the unchurched:
>
> **Monetary Christianity**
>
> In the Mennonite church some of our most satisfying work-outs take place not in gyms but at biannual Board meetings where we do our Lapps and Benders and cut back programs for the poor. They happen when we put our faith into action by choosing one program over another instead of a life of merely getting along with one another. This Sunday, write a check out to a church that will challenge you to sweat . . . to work out your budget in ways that make a difference, to us. For information on the church credit union nearest you and a free brochure on how to leave all your money to us should you die soon, call 1-900-MBM-CASH."

• • • • •

Another experiment taught us that as a small church agency, we probably should also not attempt to take on big companies like Disney or Marvel.

Again, I don't remember if the idea to follow up the two *Newsweek* ads came up at a general staff meeting on marketing and print opportunities, or if Ken brought it up with me in a one-on-one.

**Muscular Christianity**

In the Mennonite Church some of our most satisfying work-outs take place not in gyms but in the yards of hurricane victims and the homes of the poor.

Satisfaction happens when you put Christian faith into action by choosing a life of giving, instead of a life of merely getting.

This Sunday, check out a church that will challenge you to sweat . . . to work out your faith in ways that make a difference.

**For information on the church nearest you and a free book on putting faith in action call**

**800-462-8866**

**The Mennonite Churches**

Our Family Can Be Your Family

*People either loved or frowned on the "Muscular Christianity" ad published in six states in* Newsweek *in 1993. Brian Lewis conceived the copy and directed the photography.*

Ken was itching for another big publicity opportunity for the Mennonite churches. After the muscle man ad, he wanted a killer of an ad, if that's not an oxymoron for Mennonites. We would get the same Richmond firm to design the ad that had come up with "Muscular Christianity."

Eventually we built the ad on a superhero theme with the headline "Meet a Real-Life Caped Crusader." We targeted a pre-Christmas issue in late 1990. It contained the message, "This Christmas give your children superheroes they can really depend on."

The photo featured a He-Man action figure (remember him?), a Teenage Mutant Ninja Turtle Raphael, GI Joe, Master Splinter (also Teenage Mutant Ninja) and Flashback.

With that list, what made us think there wouldn't be anyone fussing about copyright infringement?

Maybe because we were meek and gentle Mennonites, if a little naïve and unassuming.

The ad was designed for Mennonite churches to use in their own local papers, and a version of the ad was supposed to run in an issue of *Newsweek* right before Christmas.

Two weeks before Christmas, we received word that even though the ad had earlier received approval by *Newsweek's* editorial board, the magazine's legal department was nervous about the ad because of (obvious) trademark concerns. Ken had the ad cleared for publication by our own legal counsel, which was told only about Media Ministries using the ad for non-profit, educational purposes. The clock continued ticking.

Ken had our firm contact *Newseek's* legal counsel, which responded that if Media Ministries was "willing to enter into an indemnification agreement that would hold *Newsweek* harmless," it would run the ad.

But Media Ministries' legal counsel advised against that. We settled for the fact that some 85 congregations ordered the holiday ad for their local use, and that 60 percent of them planned to run the ad more than once during the two weeks prior to Christmas. A pastor was quoted as praising the effort, "The ad seemed to be something that would attract people's attention—both children and adults," said a pastor from Goshen, Indiana. "Its message was [about] the birth of Christ."

At least having the ad in local papers didn't manage to attract the attention of Mattel and Hasbro. Whew.

• • • • •

At the beginning of this book I said that when I first took the job at Mennonite Broadcasts, Inc., I wasn't thinking of more than a five-year stint at one company. Didn't people usually move up or move on, even if things were going perfectly well? Did people think I was a stick in the mud, an old hand who should maybe move on? What would happen if I asked for a sabbatical? I knew going back to school for a more advanced degree would be an option, but I still didn't know what I would focus graduate studies on.

And wasn't it more important to write things that people read—rather than dissertations or theses, which were squirreled away in an academic library somewhere, with no more than four or five people ever wading through the paper? I pondered again, gratefully, the newspaper column Margaret Foth had bequeathed to me, which was still being used by a dozen or more papers. I had also been able to find publishers (a few mainstream) for the handful of books I had written—mainly out of materials first written on the job through the newspaper column or other projects. Not huge sales, but enough to keep my interest in writing books whetted. My boss, and our business manager, Lowell Hertzler, always looked at these endeavors as a way to share good content a second or third time. I know they also always hoped to birth perhaps another bestseller like those penned by David Augsburger and Ella May Miller—back in the day.

I had had three maternity leaves over the years, to be sure—in each case three months off to adjust to motherhood. By this time I was only working about three quarter's time. The breaks were refreshing but maybe I needed a new challenge to stay current in my job.

What if we innovated a "professional internship" where maybe I could work in another communications office for three months or so, just to learn from other organizations or businesses. Thus I made a proposal to Ken regarding purpose, experiences sought, and if my salary could continue. I contacted several women I knew at a women's organization in our town, and Virginia Press Women, which I was a member of for over 25 years.

Eventually I contacted a woman who was in charge of corporate communications for one of our area's largest poultry companies, known at the time as WLR Foods (Wampler Longacre Foods). When Gail Price heard about my interest in volunteering as a media intern for their company, she eagerly put me to work. I was given an out-of-date computer, and a makeshift office with a window that looked out on the poultry processing plant. That means where chickens and turkeys are killed, and prepared for market all across the U.S. Occasionally real chicken feathers floated into the upstairs room where I was located and onto my desk. Once again, I was *almost* working in a chicken house.

I learned much from Gail and her assistant, Linda Depoy. Gail kept a change of clothes, high heels and make up in her office closet, so if anything important happened, she would be ready to appear on TV or radio as a spokesperson for the company. It was also my first time working where a boss was sometimes literally waiting and looking over my shoulder for me to finish a news release. She would sometimes edit heavily. But she was always antsy to have us begin faxing it out to the media. That was extremely stressful and I was happy for my calmer work environment at Mennonite Media. But a fun thing was when Thanksgiving rolled around, it was WLR Foods' turn to decide on a farmer with an eligible turkey to receive the annual "presidential pardon" and live out its life on a farm instead of appearing on the White House's festive holiday table.

I also got to help with a photo shoot for the company magazine, where WLR Foods brought in a photographer who, the day or so before, had been photographing the presidential family—Bill, Hillary, and Chelsea Clinton—and now was taking my photo.

WLR Foods had different terminology than my office used in reference to producers. They were talking about the folks who did the hard work of raising turkey and chickens, rather than folks who make videos, ads and radio spots.

In late December, I returned to Mennonite Media—refreshed. I shared a memo with staff on the learnings I had experienced at WLR Foods, which could be applied to our work at Mennonite Media. I was glad I had long ago learned, at Mennonite Media, never to take editing of my work personally. When there are jobs to be done, one must separate any critique, helpful feedback, or edits as "just business." You want to help the business or ministry succeed so let it flow off your back.

CHAPTER 11

# What Is the Mennonite Tractor of Choice?

For those of us born in the decades before 1995, the World Wide Web brought a revolution to our lives and the world.

For our website manager for many years, Russ Neufeld, it was all "a piece of cake." He may have had to work 14 hours straight on a fix, but when you asked him to do something, the answer nine times out of ten was: "Piece of cake."

Eventually he was asked to also be the webmaster for all of Mennonite Mission Network and probably more I don't know about. His mind loved figuring out detailed messes.

Let me back up a minute.

Third Way Café[5] was launched in the middle of the early years of the Internet revolution—the "dot-com" bubble that ran roughly from 1995 to 2001. Third Way was not the first Mennonite website.

---

5 Over the years, Third Way as a domain name was frequently in demand by other businesses or organizations using the name Third Way. They were always politely turned down. Eventually in 2019, a company offered enough money that the domain name www.thirdway.com was sold, and the domain name was changed back to www.thirdwaycafe.com for the Mennonite site. (Currently, Wikipedia comes up most frequently as the place to get info on Mennonites. Many Mennonite contributors have tweaked the entries and information there.)

Mennonite Media took its time, doing research first. Mennolink started as an e-mail list/listserve in 1992 and "Mennonite Connections on the World Wide Web" began around 1995. By 1998, most Mennonite organizations, and some churches, had fledgling websites.

But before jumping into this evolving medium, Ken wanted to get the support of pastors and congregations. He organized a series of consultations in key Mennonite communities in 1997 seeking to establish a website that would "help the church be relevant and effective in carrying out its mission using the contemporary media of the age." I think most of us who participated (I helped with one in Ohio) were thinking, "enough already." We were like the Israelites begging for a king in the time of Samuel—the church was ready for what other people had—a modern website.

Jerry Holsopple took a study sabbatical to learn HTML coding at Georgetown University near Washington, D.C., commuting several days a week. His experiences there and overall artsy creativity led to the first installment of a website. He campaigned strongly to name it Third Way Café, connecting to Mennonite/Anabaptist faith as neither fully Protestant nor Catholic, but a "third" alternative way.

A bit deeper background. For years as Mennonite Media produced messages that were in the public media, on radio or TV, we posted and shared addresses for people to write to—longhand snail mail. Eventually we had an 800 number people could call free. Usually, they wrote or called about a specific program or radio spot content, but occasionally they would ask more general questions about Mennonites.

In the Vision '95 era when we moved into more print public media activities, we released ads that attempted to dispel myths about Mennonites. We also released Mennonite videos on networks like the Odyssey TV channel.

Because we had people asking a lot of questions about Mennonites, we created a basic brochure to describe Mennonites in non-churchy, non-historian, non-theological language. We started by adapting one that had been written earlier by Wilbert Shenk, an outstanding theology and missiology guy. I shepherded it through about 15 drafts and numerous revisions, more every time we went back to print. With that brochure and 800 number, we also received more calls and letters asking about Mennonites. That was some of the vision evolving from our work in public media, so we were elated when the website was finally launched in 1998.

Third Way Café soon occupied a number one spot on many major search engines. We first went online with six topic areas and one hundred or so early pages. We received a total of 432 questions about Mennonites, churches and beliefs during the 1998 fiscal year from all sources (phone, mail, email). There were 164 requests to find the closest Mennonite church, while another 95 had questions about Mennonite beliefs. Thirty-eight inquiries were from students seeking help on papers, ranging from elementary to post graduate, but we soon edged away from "writing papers" for students and encouraged them to do their own research.

To help people identify where Mennonite churches could be found, for a while we used the MennoLocater computer software innovated by Tim Lichti for the Mennohof Visitor Center in Shipshewana, Indiana. It was a wonderful advancement at the time, listing churches by zip code area, making it easier to match the zip code of the inquirer with the zip code of a church.

One of my favorite early stories arising out of Third Way was the account of Todd and Andrea Grotenhuis, two young adults who liked what they found not only at Third Way Café, but at a local Mennonite church.

Todd, an information security specialist, and Andrea, a chemist, both in their mid-20s, did lots of research on churches over a period of years. Both of them have Protestant roots but became interested in finding a local church that more closely matched their beliefs. When they were looking for a new church home in Indianapolis, Indiana, Todd checked out Third Way.

"Sometimes it is hard to get basic beliefs out of a denomination," Todd said, because "beliefs are a touchy subject and groups almost 'hide' them." But at Third Way, he was delighted with what he found, particularly: "a clear statement about what is commonly believed. I appreciated the honesty and openness. It is hard enough to look for a church, but this was a good resource and I found it matched my beliefs."

Todd said while the introduction included a general disclaimer that some churches are different than others, "It gave me a starting point." The Grotenhuises became active participants at First Mennonite Church in Indianapolis, even though Andrea also maintained membership in her home Presbyterian congregation.

Other early finders were Paul and Sarah Hebblethwaite who in 1998 were a young couple desiring a church home and committed Christian discipleship. After finding Third Way, they also discovered the Mennonite Voluntary Service program and served a term in Fresno, California. Later, they both ended up being employed by the organizations they served there, Paul at an HIV-AIDS family facility of the Salvation Army, and Sarah completing seminary studies at Fuller Theological Seminary. Eventually, the Hebblethwaites gravitated to Pasadena Mennonite Church. They said they learned from the leadership style there and enjoyed the incorporation of liturgical worship styles.

At the ten-year point (2008) after launch, Third Way Café was offering more than 3,000 pages of Mennonite information, audio files, video clips and downloadables, essays, reviews, scriptures, and conversation. Mennonite Media also created seven additional ministry websites on specific social issues since then.

Here are samples of numerous true questions people asked. They range from the sublime, to the (arguably) ridiculous. It seems that many today still have huge confusion about Mennonites and Amish, and likely never heard of Anabaptists. Some names have been withheld.

1. WHERE WAS I BAPTIZED? "I was baptized by immersion by a Bishop (Jacob)? Martin, from the Kitchener area in the early 1940s, together with several siblings, but have no record of it. The baptism took place in Fraser Lake, near Fort Stewart, Ontario. I believe my brother Daniel and a sister Faythe were the other two baptized at that time. Our parents are both dead and there are no certificates to be found." – Ernest

2. A MORTGAGE THE SAME AS USURY? A caller wanted guidance on whether Mennonites think that since in a normal mortgage you pay about 2-3 times the price of the loan in interest, whether that equates to the biblical "usury" practice that persons were urged to avoid, and whether a 401K is gambling.

3. NEED MENNONITE INTERPRETER FAST. A staff person from a language interpretation office for a state employment office, which does interpretation by telephone, needed a "Mennonite interpreter" by the following day. Someone who came to them needing services said his language was "Mennonite." Mennonite Media referred them to the Lancaster Mennonite Information Center due to the many speakers of Pennsylvania Dutch in that area.

4. ARE MENNONITES PUNCTUAL OR LATE? "What do Mennonites believe about their personal space and the use of touch in that setting? Are Mennonites usually punctual or late to appointments? Are they past, present or future oriented? What do Mennonites think about exercise, work…?" – Bethany

5. MENNONITES AND MAPLE SYRUP DISEASE. "I am just learning about a disease called Maple Syrup Urine Disease. I found that this mostly happens among Mennonites. So now I am also learning about them as well. I wondered if you could tell me more about their beliefs and how they live? Also, do you know why this disease is so common among these people?" – Tara

6. NOT OBVIOUS QUESTIONS. "Is the Bible Mennonites use the same as any other? Can a head covering be worn with regular clothes by a Protestant? Do you 'convert' or just decide to become

Mennonite? If there isn't a church around, can you teach yourself? Does a Mennonite have to go a Mennonite church? Sorry if these are obvious questions, but I really don't know anything about it, so thanks!" – Stephanie

7. MENNONITES AND STEM CELL RESEARCH. "My daughter, who is a sophomore in high school, is in a debate about stem cell research. I was wondering if you have anything or can direct her to websites with Mennonite perspectives about this issue." – Christine

8. PUPPY MILLS. "In the past I have held the Mennonites in the highest esteem. Your devotion to God and simplicity is wonderful. You have had a reputation for peace and gentleness. It has come to me that there is a problem in your midst. I don't know if it is an approved undertaking, or if individuals are responsible, but I hear that there are groups of Mennonites that run puppy mills. Any time animals such as faithful dogs, are kept in cages piled high with droppings and feet falling through large wire mesh, there is a problem. ... Two words come to mind, greed and callousness. In my opinion, these are not words that should come up when people think of Mennonites and Christians." – Kathleen

9. SPIRITUAL MATURITY. "I have read most of your website. It's very interesting. I am a seminary student and investigating three different communities, the 16th century Mennonites being one, as to how they saw spiritual maturity develop a biblically functioning community. Any ideas for original writings would be best." – John

10. SHUNNED FAMILY. "Can the third generation of a shunned family return to the Mennonites?" – Thomas

11. MENNONITES AND CONFLICT. "I am looking for information on how the Mennonites resolve conflicts. I am currently doing a study as a research associate with the Center for Conflict Resolution in Salisbury, Maryland. My main focus is to compare the various conflict resolution techniques used by different faiths." – Tim

12. SIMPLE LIFESTYLE IN TODAY'S WORLD. "How should a Mennonite discern and understand the simple lifestyle in today's world? How do we maintain this lifestyle in our home? These questions are very important to me." – Mary

13. CATHOLIC PASTOR LOOKING FOR SIMPLE LIFE RESOURCES. "I am Father Rick (Utah) and was told by someone recently that the Mennonite community had some good resources for helping people adopt more 'simplified lifestyles.' Could you possibly direct me to some related information?" – Rick

14. WANTS TO TALK. "Over the years I have been drawn to Mennonites. I don't know why. Could you please tell me who to contact near where I live to talk about Mennonite beliefs?" – Pam

15. Y U R CALLED MENNONITES? [All original spelling] "I would like to know why y u r called Mennonites and were it started. Thank U." – Lynzz

16. LOOKING FOR MENNONITES. "I live in an isolated rural community 225 miles from the nearest Mennonite church. Recently I tried to bind myself with a Mennonite Church in several locations. Because of the distance factor the congregations were less than enthusiastic. How does one such as myself who wishes to become a Mennonite and share a faith community, proceed?" – Thom

17. NEVER HEARD OF THEM BEFORE. "I am doing a project for school. I chose the Mennonites because I knew truly nothing about them, never even heard of them, so now I need some extra information if it's no trouble." – Bethani

18. MENNONITES AND PRIVACY ISSUES. A reporter in Missouri wondered if there were Mennonite groups concerned about pending legislation in that state regarding everyone having to have a photo on their driver's license or ID card and how this impacts those with religious scruples against photos.

19. WHAT DO YOU CALL A MENNONITE CLERGY? "What is the proper form of address for a member of the Mennonite or Anabaptist clergy? Is it Pastor, Reverend, or something else?

Your prompt response would be appreciated. We have a Mennonite clergyman giving the invocation at an upcoming meeting and want to be able to include his proper title in the agenda." – from Tucson

20. RULES ON MARRIAGE. "Are Mennonites allowed to get married?" – Jeff

• • • • •

But the nature of the web is that it is constantly changing. Today people ask Alexa or Siri, or voice their own question into a smart phone.

The nice thing about email or online is the anonymity—-people can ask questions they might never dare to ask at an information center.

The drawback is also the anonymity—no accountability. We had no idea whether the person is genuine, no way of continuing a contact unless the person chose to. We tried to refer people to local Mennonite churches whenever possible, and for a while, reported those to Mennonite churches in case people showed up! But basically, staff used the website to encourage people to find an active connection to a local Mennonite (or other) church if they were serious about following Jesus. A man from New Zealand communicated with us frequently as he longed to have a local Mennonite/Anabaptist connection, and shared word about Mennonites through his local newspaper there. He had been to the U.S. several times, met Mennonites here, and was delighted to have Third Way as a touchstone for him and persons living far away from any local congregation. You could say Third Way was a digital church before we'd heard much about such.

The website was able to provide answers to frequently asked questions, and thus save a lot of time and repetition of sending the same or similar responses repeatedly. Over the years, various staff persons or contractors responded to the questions by email, letter, and sometimes phone beginning with Eva Stauffer way way back, Marian Bauman, Ruth Ann Miller, Erma Brunk, Minnette Hostetler, and Jodi

Nisly Hertzler, along with yours truly. Eventually we worked with Jodi to put together a book, *Ask Third Way Café: 50 Common and Quirky Questions about Mennonites* published by Cascadia Publishing House.

From our experience answering questions forwarded to us from Mennonite Church headquarters, Mennolink and other places, we found that some of the most frequently asked questions were these and more, still featured at Third Way. And no, there's no automatic virtual pop-up person online who answers questions in a digital dialogue box. Next iteration!

How did the Mennonite Church begin?

What do Mennonites believe about participating in war?

What's the difference between Mennonites and Amish?

What do Mennonites believe about the Bible?

What do Mennonites believe about death and dying?

What is worship like in a Mennonite church?

Where is the closest Mennonite church?

Do Mennonites have their own schools?

Can you help me trace my family tree? (No.)

What are the basic Mennonite beliefs?

What is the relationship between the terms "Anabaptist" and "Mennonite?"

Another list I dubbed the *infrequently* asked questions, include some of my personal favorites:

1. Do Mennonites have one charismatic "leader" who is elected and to whom Mennonites bow?

2. Do Mennonites encourage their children to use their imagination and pretend play? I heard it was discouraged.

3. Does any branch of the Mennonite Church believe in the purification of the races?

4. Can African Americans join the Mennonite Church?

5. I had a dream about people from Lancaster County. How can I contact them?

6. Do Mennonites believe in having age differences between spouses?

7. What is the Mennonite stance on birth control?

8. I am a Catholic male wanting to date a Mennonite female at Penn State. What is the Mennonite practice regarding relationships outside of the Mennonite Church?

9. We are having a baby and want to name it Menno. What does it mean?

10. Can you give me names of Montana log home builders who are Mennonite?

11. Where is the closest Mennonite church to me in Nevada?

12. How does the ban function today?

13. Do you feel that only Anabaptists are going to be saved, and how does Israel fit into the picture?

14. What significance does the Virgin Mary have in the Mennonite faith?

15. Should Christians pray about trivial things, such as for the porridge not to boil and the baby not to cry and the girlfriend to call?

16. What are coverings made out of? (From *The Washington Post*!)

17. What is the Mennonite position on endowed churches? (from *The Wall Street Journal*)

18. What is the Mennonite tractor of choice?

Finally, and in this day of churches combining, came a question asking about new alignments:

> How does a congregation align with the Mennonite Church? Is it possible to be dually aligned—with two or three other denominations—particularly with Baptists, Quakers, Brethren, or Disciples of Christ?

• • • • •

After Jerry left our staff, Russ Neufeld was hired to be the coding brain behind the whole site and each new development. When he started he was truly just a kid—early 20s—doing part-time audio work in our studio while he finished a degree in physics at the university across town. But even then, his gift to us was frequently responding to almost every request for change, innovation, or a new section for the website as noted earlier, "A piece of cake!" He had a brilliant mind for the job, and dedication to the Mennonite Church. He and his wife eventually moved to Newton, Kansas, where he continued working at Mennonite headquarters there.

We were all dumbfounded when we learned he had lymphoma in 2016. We could barely believe it, even though cancer had struck others in his family. He was so young, so promising. Russ endeavored to learn all he could about his illness and the various treatments available, describing on Facebook exactly how this chemo thing works anyway, in terms of the chemistry.

Who does that when they're fighting cancer? Russ Neufeld. He said it was his way of dealing with it. He did everything the doctors and experts knew to do, and then some. One could even say Russ beat his cancer, even though he did not survive. One Facebook post said Russ did not let cancer define him, destroy him, or his family.

When I read his obituary, I stared at his birth year, 1977. That hit me. I was already working in my current job before this kid was even born. Nothing fair about that. Why should a 40-year-old father of two kids just 10 and 12 be whisked away in the prime of life when many of us far older are still tinkering around? As coworkers, we were always in awe of his geeky techno know-how, his carefree joie de vie, not to mention his ability to let ideas just spin around in his head as he did endless workarounds to make something work.

Russ worked as our webmaster roughly from 2000-2010, some of those years in Harrisonburg and some from Newton. In the early days he learned html coding and used whatever other tools he could grab online (before the days when non-techies could get a website ready to go just by signing on to WordPress or Blogspot). Russ showed us how he could take over our computers from a distance to fix or demonstrate something—a surreal feeling when another hand is guiding your cursor around the screen.

We can only ponder now what kind of view Russ has of our computers and indeed our puny lives as he's off exploring a whole new reality.

*Jodi Nisly Hertzler served a number of years responding to questions sent to the Third Way Café website, and was asked to compile a book of "best" or most interesting questions, along with her responses.*

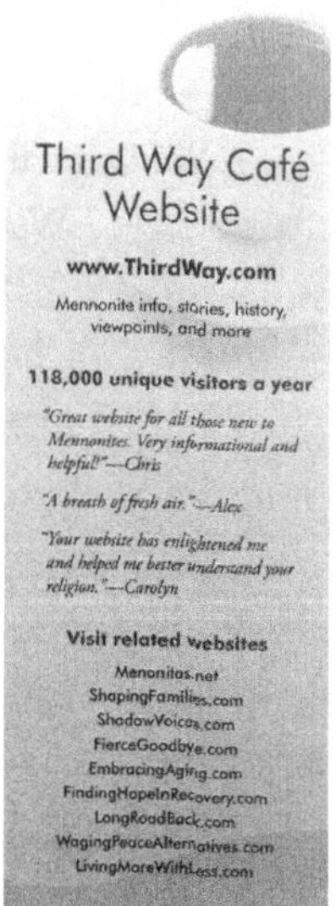

CHAPTER 12

# Office Life From Dictaphone to Rap

"Let me tell ya'll a story 'bout a guy named Zac..." rapped a young English teacher with amazing rhythm and charisma, one Brian Wasko. Our recording studio engineer wondered if some cassettes Wasko was working on in the studio (before CDs, M3Ps, YouTube) would be something we'd want to offer to churches for their youth and middle schoolers.

Ken as director gave the project a green light, but he was supportive about most new media vehicles. My younger daughters weren't even in school yet but my elementary age daughter so loved the catchy rhythms and Bible stories as told by Wasko she remembers many lines to this day. One rap, "Give what you've got" (generally on Christian stewardship) became a music video included on one of our *All God's People* videos.

So although Ken was definitely a man who tried to stay current with technology and trends in society and the church, we sometimes teased him that it was time to get rid of his Dictaphone and join the computer generation. He was slow to take up a keyboard, never having learned to type. He found the "hunt and peck" method unbearably slow going, compared to voicing a memo or letter into a mic (and having his administrative assistant type it). She of course sent real paper memos and letters to staff persons or colleagues or other church agencies on his behalf.

Ken's corner office at the end of the hall, where he could see our office driveway with people coming and going, was his perch for as long as I can remember. Before he officially retired in 1998 after 43 dedicated years, the retirement party the office had planned for him with the broader local Mennonite community had to be postponed. He suddenly needed triple bypass heart surgery, and time to recover. Thus it was delayed until spring.

• • • • •

Over the years I occupied at least eight offices at 1251 Virginia Avenue. We moved around with job changes, when new colleagues joined the staff, new programs were launched, or when two people were situated in one office and a new vacancy came up. The halls upstairs and down smelled like fresh paper and coffee—but the whiffs of paper and boxes were most noticeable in the shipping department on the basement floor.

However, about once a month for numerous years the aroma was clearly an office potluck—making it hard to work through a long morning. In the years from 2010 to 2019, staff came up with oddly themed and named potlucks: St. Patrick's Day when everyone was supposed to bring something green; breakfast-for-lunch potlucks starring some of our favorite breakfast goodies; Cinco de Mayo Day when we'd bring out the spicey deliciousness of that cuisine; or "Mystery Can" potlucks where the day before we picked up a tin can contributed by someone else with no label, took it home, and tried to come up with a delicious dish featuring the canned item—and whatever else we might pull from our shelves at home. Yes, many hours were spent in the kitchen those days, checking on casseroles or crockpots, but the camaraderie and fellowship built was precious and revered.

Only one of my other colleagues managed to stay put in a single office for all the years I worked there—and that was Lowell Hertzler, our business manager. He also took care of so many odd jobs around the building and organization that it just made sense for his door to be the first one you came to entering from the back doorway. No one budged Lowell out of his space—but he was a trooper who willingly tackled many behind-the-scenes jobs, including shoveling snow sometimes.

That one doorway was also our main entrance for probably the last 20 or so years that I worked at Mennonite Media, due to cordoning off part of the first floor of the building. We rented it out to Park View Credit Union until, years later, they built their own space. Several restaurants also sent up yummy scents for a period of 10 to 12 years. As Mennonite Media continually downsized, we needed less and less space. Plus, rental income was a blessing.

For most of my tenure, I worked on the second floor. My view included a grain elevator interrupting the skyline, which spanned the small Massanutten Range of mountains to the east, and part of the larger Blue Ridge Mountains threading down to the Smokies. Including the years I lived on or near campus at nearby Eastern Mennonite College/University, it was my neighborhood for almost 47 years. No wonder the office truly felt like "home." How would I feel when it came time to leave this second home—whether I was let go, decided to work elsewhere, or (gulp) retire?

After growing up on flat northern Indiana farmland, I never tired of being able to look up from my desk and shift my gaze to the gorgeous Shenandoah Valley on a clear day. If it was cloudy, we couldn't see the mountains. So I jabbered to the squirrels who darted on and off the window ledge and chased each other up and down in the oaks outside my second-story window.

I also relished intense conversations with squirrels and birds in nearby Park Woods, which I savored walking in over the years, mainly at lunchtime. I should add that this didn't happen much in the years when our three daughters were young—because lunch hours were great times to run errands, since the girls' activities and supervision took precedence in after-work hours. Michelle, Tanya, and Doreen were born in 1981, 1983 and 1986, respectively, and all finished their high school years by 2004. After 2004 I began my walks in earnest, often going a mile.

• • • • •

So my office was my second home and my first boss became a role model for not only how to lead an organization, but how to leave graciously whenever the time came. Ken worked past the typical retirement time of 65 and took his retirement at age 67. He did so with great courtesy and levelheadedness, leaving the bones of a solid organization, even though finances were a continual struggle.

I never envied him his position. I wouldn't have wanted the difficult work of deciding when to lay someone off, or close down a whole program, but he seemed to manage the stress of those decisions with equilibrium intact. Over the years, Mennonite Media housed the Choice Books organization, which went on its own in 1998; and cut ties with Spanish language programming in South America as well as Puerto Rico where his own brother-in-law had been instrumental in its broadcast work. We also eventually cut ties with most other international radio programs that had flourished at one point—the Mennonite Media budget would only stretch so far and the reasoning went: If locals there had not invested heavily enough to keep the programming going, why should an agency from afar do so? I didn't always agree with that philosophy and the cuts hurt, but Ken, with the backing of the board, did what he needed to do.

One of the biggest changes Ken pulled off with the help of an eager and willing Choice Books team was their move out of the Mennonite Media building (in city limits) and taking on their own structure. This was partially because they had become so large and profitable as a ministry that it didn't quite fit our non-profit status any longer. John Bomberger was hired as director in 1993 and by 1997 they were selling two million books a year. They decided to move their headquarters to Rockingham County, which changed their tax liability as well. This raised the question of what would happen to the huge warehouse we'd built in the 80s to store the Choice Books inventory (some inventory went straight from publishers' warehouses to the various Choice Books distributors across the U.S.). Thus the warehouse became rentable space to others, and income for a number of years.

The timing was certainly good for Choice Books to become an independent company; when I first joined the staff in 1975, they were selling about 500,000 a year. More importantly, their focus has always been on the ministry aspect, and it always used to make me a little proud to see those racks in airports, tourist shops, and even Walmarts all across the country. Today they average selling around 5.2 million books a year from smaller office space. Some directors perhaps would have shied away from letting such a profitable and major part of our operation move on. I don't know how Ken felt down deep—we all hated to see our friends and comrades move out—but I think he knew and sensed the wisdom of the split.

Ken was a master at keeping records and creating reports that summarized activities. He made sure our staff did the same, engaging in a two-day office-wide clean up every other year. On those days we set aside other work and meetings in order to sort through, discard, organize and send historical materials to the Mennonite Church Archives in Elkhart and Goshen, Indiana—the things that someone may want to research and know someday.[6] We were usually treated to pizza those days.

When things were sometimes discarded, I would save memos, letters, or reports that seemed worth saving. This story was collected from one of those purges. Mr. Balinder from Zondervan Press wrote, "Last night as I watched the Don Knotts Show, one of your spot

6 Online, some of Ken's work and Mennonite Media history is stored in the Mennonite Archival Commons: "Mennonite Media Director's correspondence and files 1954-1999." http://mac.libraryhost.com/?p=collections/findingaid&id=1172&q=

messages came on, saying 'God made children to be loved.' It was great—and in prime time. What a ministry!"

Ken was not perfect, either as a boss or a man, but here is a score of things I learned from Ken as a boss and executive director:

> **Research and development, or the old R & D.** Ken was a big believer (and practitioner) of always keeping some money in your budget for R & D; if you don't, it becomes that much harder to do the big innovative idea when one arises out of culture, issues at hand, or the church. Ken was instrumental in bringing the Inter Mennonite Media Group (IMMG) into being where four denominations cooperated in creating multimedia campaigns. It was a work group with projects that members could join or not join—depending on whether they had some "pin" money in their budget to put into a new project. One enormously meaningful spin off of IMMG was a professional association first called "Council on Church and Media" (CCM).
>
> Together the members of CCM produced TV spots for which they might not have had budget alone, and pulled together other multimedia campaigns. Those spots and campaigns were tagged "a production of the Mennonite churches," which encompassed all of the denominations with Mennonite in their name. Some of the projects included the Anabaptist sister group, Church of the Brethren, added to the sponsorship line. Eventually the name for the professional association was changed to Anabaptist Communicators, and I was asked to serve as chair of the group for two years. The organization still goes on, mainly online! I loved that it meant travel and inspiration from others in similar fields. Kudos to Ken for budgeting for such.

**Big ideas.** Ken was always open to the next big idea—wanting to read the latest book and quote the leading business gurus. That can sound cheesy, but he didn't do it to sound one up. He was genuinely inquisitive. One such project was the Vision Interfaith Satellite Network (look it up on Wikipedia, or see footnote on page 151). As a small denomination, we participated along with huge denominations such as the United Methodists, Episcopalians, Lutherans, and more. Later when we began producing documentaries with social/justice issues and themes, the fact that Ken had stepped up earlier to participate in the Odyssey and Hallmark ventures gave us entre to a much bigger platform. Again, he had R & D money set aside for such ventures.

**Tackle new projects.** Ken rarely said no to a new idea or involvement or to something the church asked him to do or explore. As an employee, I learned to not say no to new work projects either, which helped me survive on staff for 43+ years, such as the *Proverbs* radio project when I was little more than youth group age myself. I was asked to work on print products for Vision '95, which probably weren't the most exciting projects for either him or me. But we had an interesting time doing such, as already mentioned in this book.

**Consult, confer, come home.** He lived for meetings, and came home with a Dictaphone tape full of memos, letters, and proposals for his secretary to transcribe. Distracted driving? Maybe.

Or if driving/riding with others on a business trip, you'd have a pre- or post-car committee meeting—which he would summarize in a quickly dictated memo back in his office.

**Listen to the goals and needs of the church.** Ken was a church businessman, which meant he paid attention to the shifts and callings of the church. When pushes came along to become an antiracism church, he asked me if I would be willing to serve on that team for Mennonite Media. It didn't take much praying to say yes, and I knew my father would bless such efforts. The initial antiracism team training took weeks (at several different times), which was work time. It called me away from office and home, leaving my dear husband to fix food and manage carpools. I loved the travel and intense meetings where I learned so much about the racism that affects us all. But it was also among the most difficult work I was asked to do. I came home practically in tears from one meeting when participants couldn't come to an agreement and I despaired for the church. In jumping on this effort in the late 1990s, we were ahead of many mainline Christian denominations.

**Continue education.** Ken was a strong supporter of allowing and prioritizing continuing education benefits for everyone. When possible, he would send at least two staff to one event so they could process it together and bounce innovative ideas off each other.

**Hire kids.** He gave young kids like me, just out of college, chances to do something big, even if they turned out looking very amateur. He did the same with Jerry Holsopple, *Shalom Lifestyles: Whole People, Whole Earth*, and later, a fun and creative series of peacemaking videos for children. Ron Byler was a young and able producer for the *All God's People* discussion videos in the "video magazine" style of the day. I guess Ken sensed youthful employees can be innovators. Think of the college kid who invented Facebook.

**Don't hesitate to send your staff.** If Ken didn't have time for a certain meeting or involvement, he did not hesitate to send one of us. Along with others, I had turns representing our agency and by extension the Mennonite churches at meetings of the National Council of Churches (covered in other chapters). But our contacts and camaraderie with folks at the NCC led to great connections with the Odyssey Network while it existed, and provided sources of funds for our hour-long TV documentaries from 2000-2010.

Mennonite Media also endeavored to send a rep to the annual meeting of the American Bible Society, just to stay in touch with their communications and technology advances (such as putting the whole Bible online, when that was considered rather amazing). The year I got to go was over my birthday in early December. I found visiting the Christmas tree at Rockefeller Center one evening a perfect way to spend my birthday. On that trip I also met pastor and social activist John Perkins and shared a taxi ride with him to the airport. I later contacted and interviewed him to appear in our first documentary, *Journey Toward Forgiveness.*

**Stay accessible.** Some people call that transparency. Ken didn't talk a lot about being open and transparent, but he was. He tapped shoulders, walked into your office without an appointment, and kept, religiously, one-on-one check-in meetings with those he supervised. He also summarized key points in memos, so you knew your marching orders. But he didn't meddle, check in on progress, or micromanage, and left reporting in back on you. I was generally excited to go to these meet ups because I never knew what new or exciting projects he'd discuss with me, with travel assignments or new committee work.

**Allow entry level staff to try new things.** If you recall the beginning of this book, I was first a secretary, then a secretary-writer (and paid accordingly with split pay level), a producer, and then an executive producer. Too often, entry level folks get stymied there—more because of personnel department guidelines than from their own lack of initiative.

**Close down, let go, get out.** Ken knew when to cut his losses and close down programs; he did so mostly with grace and good feelings. Unfortunately, this is another part of innovation. Things don't always work out. Times change, things move on. He was willing to let go of things bigger than him.

**Invite staff to board meetings.** This goes against current models of board/staff relationships and working. I learned much while sitting in on or taking minutes during board meetings. Don't shut your staff out if you can at all afford it. At least have a lunch together, either catered or potluck. Staff want to feel like they know the board and have a place to turn (that transparency thing again). Staff become visible and approachable for board and vice versa.

**Don't worry if ideas fizzle.** This one I learned from a later boss, Burton Buller. He was a popcorn popper full of ideas. Sometimes they took years to bear fruit, and other times they just died in the hopper. Great ideas pop to the top.

> **Change is constant.** When I think about the era that Ken lived through and all the technical inventions and applications that came into being, we get a picture of the future. Even our scriptures end with a book of "and I saw a new heaven, and new earth." Revelation 21:1 goes on to say "for the first heaven and the first earth had passed away, and there was no longer any sea."
>
> Talk about change! We may not understand all of the prophecy but our own lives teach us not to whine for the way things were, but to accept change, move on, and walk humbly with our God.

• • • • •

We were finally able to host a fine retirement celebration for Ken in March 2000 while Mennonite Media was also hosting a joint board meeting of the Mennonite Church Mennonite Board of Missions and the General Conference Mennonite Church Commission on Oversees Missions (the two denominations merged shortly thereafter). For a guy who was Mr. Church Agency, there couldn't have been a better send off.

In early 2001, some of us were assigned to be part of larger teams in the Mennonite Church USA to help imagine what our new denomination would look like—what forms our agencies would take. What was key going forward? What could we streamline or reimagine? These were important, time-consuming meetings, often including parts of weekends—the better not to interfere with normal work assignments, I guess. My team had the assignment of program development for the new agency. Another had the assignment to work on a new name for the broader agency, and landed on Mennonite Mission Network (MMN) as the name going forward.

We met in places like Colorado, Chicago, Kansas—mostly Midwest, which was central for most participants. One meeting scheduled for April at the Sisters of Saint Francis convent in Colorado Springs was running along smoothly. Then someone noticed fluffy snow falling outside the retreat cabin. We watched with wonder and amusement at our beautiful surroundings now topped off by snow. Interesting how this part I *keenly* remember.

Then people started worrying. How long would it go on? Would we be able to fly home that evening as planned? People began grabbing their phones during breaks to check with the airport. The snow was mounting up by the foot. Our group all ended up spending the night in a motel near the airport, and flying out the next day. That evening, back at home, I saw the Denver Airport and a reporter on the evening news talking about its "snowed-in" status. I was so glad to have arrived home safely.

The new church organizations were finalized at the Nashville, Tennessee, convention in 2001, and it all became official February 1, 2002. I was asked to write a prayer litany for Mission Network as part of an office worship service and celebration.

As time rolls on—as Ken's career and gifts illustrated so amply—being ready to change and explore new ways of being were out there, waiting to be discovered.

*The inventive theme for this office potluck was "A Dark and Stormy Night."*

*Staff members (2012) enjoyed summer picnics for many years with family members invited.*

*Ken Weaver shares memories at a belated retirement banquet in his honor (postponed from his 1999 retirement due to illness), while Melodie Davis looks on.*

CHAPTER 13

# Drugs, Mental Illness, Suicide, Aging, and More

"I will go make sure our van hasn't been towed," I told videographers Wayne Gehman and Jim Bowman, although I was sure in my rural head that the van was fine. It was only two minutes after four. Street signs had told us that morning that all cars needed to be removed for purposes of commuter traffic by 4 p.m.

We were wrapping up a full day of video interviews and shooting b-roll (supplemental footage) in New York City, a thrill in itself. The guys would be putting away all of the video equipment, lights, props, and backdrops for at least an hour and there was only so much I knew how to do. I owed them the favor of going out to check on the van, even though I had not been the driver at any time that trip.

I hurried out of the retirement apartment complex with its housing, dining rooms, courtyard, activity rooms and more for senior citizens, where we had been filming all day. I walked about a block to where we'd found parking. As always on New York City streets, horns were honking, sirens screaming in the distance, and the gritty air and sidewalks filled my senses.

Then my mouth dropped open. The van was nowhere to be seen. Huh? You're kidding me! How did they tow it away that quickly? The tow truck must have had its eye on our out-of-state plates. Or had it been stolen? What to do next? I jotted down the directions from the "Tow away zone" sign on the street, which included a phone number for an impound lot.

I couldn't imagine that our vehicle would have been removed so quickly. How would I find our van in the biggest city in the U.S.?

An attendant on duty in the retirement apartments exhaled a tired sigh for this stupid woman. He handed me a piece of paper with instructions for where to go to redeem our vehicle. I jumped in an elevator to go back up to where the guys were working.

"The van's been towed!" I rolled my eyes when I saw Wayne. His mouth dropped a little. Jim cracked a smile and kept working. As a contract videographer, he wasn't responsible for the company vehicle, but Wayne and I were. None of us wanted to be without a vehicle at the end of a long but interesting work day in the Big Apple.

"Here's where the van is supposed to be," I showed Wayne the paper I'd collected. "And I *will* go get it," I said firmly. This was, I remind you again, in the days before there was GPS on everyone's phones. We had some cell phones between us, but nothing smart yet. "I'll call a cab I guess," I said. "I would hate to walk that far this time of day."

"It might actually be faster what with the traffic," Wayne shrugged. "But yeah, get a cab. Lowell shouldn't make you pay for it," he joked.

Getting a cab wasn't too hard. The compound was somewhere close to Pier 76 on the Hudson. My phone now tells me it was less than two miles away from our work, and a 10-minute drive, depending on traffic.

The tow yard looked like a scene from a bad movie where drug dealers or maybe even Mafia guys hung out. I drew in a breath, prayed, and went inside. After a long wait and staring at signage of what I was to do, I eventually completed the necessary paperwork and called our business manager, Lowell, just to check in about what had happened.

At last they gave me a small pass with our company van information on it marked "Redeemed." The Christian connotations of that word lifted me out of my fear and trepidation. I took that pass and made my way through the garage, which housed many other towed vehicles. "Whew," I breathed out when I finally spotted our van. I had the keys and it wasn't too hard to find my way back over to where the guys were, now waiting in the lobby of the retirement building with all the gear packed up and waiting on the van. I pondered whether maybe they were wondering if they'd ever see me again.

But what were we doing in New York City in the first place?

• • • • •

When Ken retired in 1999 at the age of 67, the board hired a film producer named Burton Buller to pick up the reins. While Ken was a super executive who left the creativity to others, Burton came into Mennonite Media as an artistic producer turned executive. Immediately prior to that, he had been serving as CEO of Mennonite Brethren Communications (MBC) based in Winnipeg, Manitoba. His early career was spent working for Mennonite Central Committee's photo department in Akron, Pennsylvania. Then for a number of years he was a stay-at-home dad, freelancing in various creative media endeavors.

After growing up in Nebraska, he'd become a motorcycle and boots kind of guy who didn't mind wearing blue jeans to the office if he felt like it. Plus, he had the natural to-die-for deep radio voice that David Augsburger had, making both guys shoe-ins to voice their own scripts. Burton was an aficionado of radio, film, and video—and skilled in all three. He planned to work half time for us—from a distance—and continue working half time for MBC for the next year, as one son was still finishing secondary school (high school) in Winnipeg. Burton promised our board he would explore cooperative inter-Mennonite media projects for the two agencies. Burton and his wife were working on becoming dual-citizens of the U.S. and Canada, the better to travel back and forth, especially as he hoped to continue filming in both countries in years ahead.

So it didn't surprise me that one of the first projects I worked on with Burton at the helm was a new set of radio spots. The MBC agency created some programming in Spanish, airing both in Latin American countries and North America. Mennonite Media had good raw interviews with various persons at that point from years of producing *Beyond the News* discussion videos, so I was to comb through interview scripts looking for both poignant and gut-wrenching stories on the theme of forgiveness. We planned to create a dozen or so 30-second radio spots. The spots dealt with gripping stories of people who had experienced wrongs, such as an operating room error removing the wrong breast, forgiveness after a marital affair, a daughter who was kidnapped, a father who was stabbed, a head-on crash, forgiving a killer, a woman abused. The spots encouraged listeners to think of forgiveness as a long process, allowing victims to let go of their intense emotional pain over time, and receive some measure of healing.

We also used stories from one of their Spanish-language programs for the Spanish spots, and Burton lined up a woman in the Winnipeg office to handle any Spanish-language phone calls we might receive. In early 2001, we were able to send some 8,000 CDs to "talk radio" and country music radio stations.

It felt really good to be able to send out PSAs to both U.S. and Canadian stations on this theme, and to also offer spots in the second language of many in the United States. We called the package "Forgiveness: It's Your Choice," which played on the name of our flagship "Choice" spot series by David Augsburger, which had been popular for many years.

• • • • •

A sweet after-play regarding these spots came via a writer-producer for American Communications Foundation who read about these radio spots in *Sojourners* magazine. The writer pitched the story to producers of the *Osgood Files*. Back in the day, it was a daily morning drivetime show consisting of three-minute radio commentaries. The *Osgood Files* were a radio staple, running nearly 50 years from 1971 until 2017. Charles Osgood, the voice and producer, also appeared on the CBS-TV *Sunday Morning* show from 1994 to 2016. We were ecstatic to know our Mennonite spots had drawn the attention of this longtime personality. The Osgood producer set up a time for a call back with me to record an interview, which would air at a later time.

As I waited for the phone call from Mr. Osgood's producer, I wondered why I'd ever agreed to it. At least on radio, no one would be able to see me sweat, or critique my outfit.

Our studio engineer helped hook up a telephone connection that would produce high-quality sound. Would I stammer? Would I flub a pronunciation—something I was famous for? What would he ask? Would the audio connection fail? At least it wasn't live.

I'll admit I was somewhat disappointed that I didn't actually get to converse with Mr. Osgood, but relieved it would be edited. American Communications Foundation wrote of our spots, "While they [Mennonite Media] recognize that there is less incentive for nonreligious people to forgive, they hope to raise awareness of forgiveness as a realistic option for the general population. The Mennonites' emphasis on forgiveness can be traced to certain core beliefs. Mennonites believe that one should emulate Jesus in everyday living and behavior, and that Jesus taught the way of peace. Since they believe Christians should strive to live the lessons of Christ, Christians should forgive as well."

• • • • •

After we mailed out the spots on forgiveness, some Canadian stations said they *would* have used them had they been produced in Canada. The Canadian Radio and Television Commission (CRTC) requires broadcasters to devote a percentage of air time to public service announcements (PSAs).

In the months to come, Burton jumped on that issue. He suggested I come up to Winnipeg and produce some new spots in the Mennonite Brethren (MB) studio with Canadian talent—as it is called in the industry—voices hired to read commercials or PSAs. He thought we could probably record the voices easily in one week's time, and I would stay in one of the guest rooms at Canadian Mennonite University (CMU) and take my meals (cheaply) in the cafeteria there.

"Where will I find voice talent?" I pondered out loud in one meeting. I had developed a list of local voices in Virginia, which we used, depending on our projects. But where would I start to find folks who were 1,500 miles away—in another country?

"You can email or call the engineer there, Reg Sawatzky, for some names he knows," Burton proposed. "For one, there's Marilyn Houser Hamm," Burton added. Marilyn is not only a well-known Mennonite composer, but does great voice work as well. Burton also recalled the name of Michelle Sawatzky (no relation to Reg) a member of the Canadian Olympic volleyball team that competed in Atlanta, Georgia, in 1996, and worked for Radio AM 1250 in Steinbach, Manitoba (a Mennonite-owned station).

I was excited to return to Winnipeg for a week on my own, and for the opportunity to work in another studio. Earlier, at the beginning of Burton's tenure with Mennonite Media, he had arranged for all our work team leaders to travel to Winnipeg to meet our new cohorts at MBC.

"I want you to meet the Mennonite Brethren staff and have a good old MB prayer meeting," Burton winked, knowing their style of prayer and worship was perhaps a little more evangelical than most Mennonite Church U.S. churches. "And you'll learn how we live in -20 degree temperatures," he joked.

"How do you even start your cars in such temperatures?" someone asked.

"Well, we've gotten in the habit of not turning them off very much on such days, just leave them run!" That sounded really strange but was apparently true.

With his wife Mary, Burton invited us to breakfast at their home. Mary showed us the basket of slippers we could don (keeping our own socks on) as soon as we entered their home, a custom most people observed throughout Canada she said, and of course many other countries of the world. The breakfast, mostly made by Burton, was delightfully delicious with freshly ground hazelnut coffee, if I remember correctly. Our meeting lasted most of the morning.

So, return to Winnipeg? In a hot minute! Sign me up!

But there was a lot of work to do first. Landing on a theme for a new set of spots. Scripts. Lining up talent. Arranging schedules, studio time, getting enough Canadian currency to last a week. At least passports weren't required at that time.

• • • • •

My second night back in Winnipeg, Burton and Mary treated me to dinner at a lovely high-end restaurant. After we ordered hors d'oeuvres, a snail in garlic sauce sat staring at me on a small China plate.

With sudden bravery and since they were paying, I had allowed them to order the *escargot* bourguignon that I probably wouldn't have tried if I'd even found a restaurant serving it in Harrisonburg. But I think a desire to appear citified and sophisticated led me to sink my teeth in. It was delightful! My mind flashed back to another unusual seafood consumed almost on a dare by my Spanish professor the year I lived in Spain—fried calamari or squid. Squid and snail, they were both delicious, even if I never ever ordered them again. Maybe once was enough.

We called the radio spots "Parenting on the Edge," which promised to tackle tough issues. Topics included the difficulty of parents combining work with extra-curricular activities like soccer, with giving children quality time—talking about sex with children, the "hook up" culture, a son coming out to parents, dealing with divorce, etc. A Spanish writer/voice talent, Lourdes Alcaniz, and MBC engineer Jorge Ramirez put together the Spanish spots. The most fun thing we did was hire about four children from a local Winnipeg theater group—who auditioned for the opportunity, and provided authentic kid voices for the spots featuring children. And yes, we got to work with the Olympian Mennonite volleyball player—who at this writing affirmed she has been working for Radio 1250 in Steinbach for 25 years.

The spots went on to win an award in the 2003 Gracie Allen Awards (named for the long ago radio and TV star) from the American Women in Radio and Television. Their award dinner came complete with red carpet treatment at a New York City hotel. I think the topics we approached as a church agency, along with offering counterpart spots in Spanish, were what enabled me to bring home our agency's first "Gracie."

An additional radio project I got to spearhead was one we called *Postcards from Nazareth*, fifteen 90-second radio spots and two 30-minute Christmas specials produced and written by a tour guide at Nazareth Village in the Middle East. This idea came largely from the imaginative powerhouse, Mike Hostetler, who with his wife Virginia helped locals there create the Nazareth Village open air museum. The tour guide made the stories of Jesus come alive. We contracted with a local Virginia radio station owner and broadcaster David Eshleman (who paid most of his own expenses) to travel to Nazareth to tape those beautiful stories as told by the tour guide. Burton was pleased that this "one off" package of programs was used by perhaps 40-50 U.S. stations over several Christmas seasons.

• • • • •

It was not too surprising that early in Burton's tenure with Mennonite Media, he came back from a communications committee meeting of the National Council of Churches[7] (NCC) in New York City with stirring news. The NCC organization had given its blessing for the Mennonite Church to pursue producing one of the *Vision and Values* series of documentaries, which were airing on ABC-TV. The NBC network also aired a series called *Horizons of the Spirit,* also as a nod to religious programming produced by interfaith groups. This news was exhilarating and a bit daunting. This programming was a far cry from—and a religious alternative to—the televangelists of the 80s and 90s such as Jerry Falwell, Pat Robertson, and Jim and Tammy Bakker.

The original documentary pitch Burton made to that communications committee was on the theme of dealing with end-of-life issues. But the longer we wrestled with that theme, we came to land on how very difficult it was to deal with death and dying when a loved one has been murdered, killed by a drunk driver or terrorist bombing, and other excruciatingly tough circumstances.

"What would you think of trying your hand researching and pre-interviewing persons with potential stories?" Burton asked, looking at me. My heart started racing. That sounded interesting, exciting and scary. But initially I was like a deer in headlights, looking for a way to run. Burton continued by saying that eventually I would help sketch out a direction for the scripting of the documentary and write voice-over or announcer copy for the narrator.

---

[7] Ken Weaver had the foresight to begin participating in meetings of the Vision Interfaith Satellite Network (1988-1992) on behalf of Mennonite Media, because he sought ever wider networking and exposure for our work; another group, American Christian Television System (1984-1992) combined to create VISN/ACTS, which soon was renamed the Faith & Values Channel from 1993-1996. A separate Odyssey Network ran from 1996-2001 and was absorbed into the Hallmark Channel. This all led to working with the Interfaith Broadcasting Commission to air our documentaries on NBC-TV in their *Horizons of the Spirit* series, and on *Vision and Values,* an ABC-TV series, and helped us secure some production grants.

Was I really up to that kind of writing? Of course there would be plenty of others weighing in with editing, both on paper and then in the final video cuts. The main message we wanted to deliver was shaped by a whole team of people and months of research, interviewing, and writing.

I think I said I'd have to think about it. I prayed, too, seriously wondering how on earth I could do it. Wasn't I busy enough already? But what an opportunity!

Of course I said yes and with heart racing, jumped into calling people I would never have had the nerve or opportunity to just call up on the phone: John Perkins, the crusader for people of color or those living below the poverty line; the father of a teenager killed by a drunk driver; a couple whose daughter was kidnapped, then murdered. These people were quickly interested in my random call when I told them I was doing background research for a documentary that was to air on ABC-TV. "Network TV" seemed to be a magic key that unlocked our access.

I had to call a man whose daughter was killed in the Oklahoma City terrorist bombing in April 1995. Bud Welch was willing to talk—always eager to share his deeply held and hard-won belief that he had to forgive the bomber in order to survive the death of his 23-year-old daughter in that tragedy. If you recall, 167 others had died at the hands of the bomber, Timothy McVeigh.

We worked on the show in the months leading up to 9-11. Yes, September 11, 2001.

The work was exhilarating, frustrating, mind-bending, and full of can-I-really-do-this questions. I knew there would be Burton, Jerry, Sheri, and Wayne adding their own touches and expertise, especially when it came to editing the actual video interviews, where nuances come alive with the eyes, the mouth, the turn of a head, the long pause, the tears that rise and ebb and sometimes fall from the interviewees.

There were dead ends, wrong turns, and I got stuck. Numerous times. But we kept plowing away, months and months on one key project, while keeping my other assignments going for Mennonite Media. Newsletters, news releases, quarterly and annual reports, emails—these held no candle to working on a documentary to air on national TV.

The final result was an award-winning tribute to these heroes who had survived unthinkably tragic circumstances of their loved ones' deaths. In all cases but one, they had gotten to the place in their hearts that they wanted to forgive the perpetrator, or die a slow and terrible inner death themselves. By late August, the program was almost ready for its early December airing on stations in the ABC-TV network (which individual stations could choose to use or not use).

Then September 11 happened. Like almost everyone else, I can certainly remember what I was doing when I heard the terrible news. I was talking to one of my media mentors, Ruth Brunk Stoltzfus, giving feedback on her memoir she was working on. Our webmaster, Russ Neufeld, came around to my office and others, telling us that a plane had just flown into the World Trade Center in New York City.

In 2001, most of us did not spend most of our days hooked to smart phones and social media or browsing the Internet but of course Russ was online because of his job and picked up the news there. Ruth and I quickly finished up, she left, and barely knowing what to believe or understand, I went downstairs to where the office TV was already on in the assembly room.

The world stood still and our lives were changed forever—almost another Pearl Harbor—as we began to comprehend the truth and reality of the attack. We sat there and watched news announcers trying to make sense out of what had just happened and listened to rumors of what else might be happening. An attack on the White House? The Pentagon? A rogue plane somewhere in western Pennsylvania? We couldn't speak. What was going on? Our office was situated only two hours outside of Washington, D.C. Was there an attack coming our way? Our minds raced as we looked at each other and more and more staff trickled in to watch the footage.

Our planned and almost-finished documentary called *Journey Toward Forgiveness* was to open with footage from the previously worst domestic disaster: the Oklahoma City bombing. It was a horrible and gut-wrenching scene still fresh in the national psyche. But without even checking with ABC-TV, we felt compelled to change our opening sequence for the documentary. We moved the Oklahoma story further into the program, so that it would not immediately bring to mind the recent September 11 catastrophes with more than 3,000 deaths. It was definitely too soon to even broach the topic of true forgiveness, yet there were such raw and painful stories there in our documentary that would perhaps begin to speak and sow the seeds that would later lead to healing for the families and friends of the many victims. That did indeed happen with time, for some people.

The phones at our office lit up during the show as it aired that December, and as soon as the program finished, our lines were flooded. It had initially aired on just a few stations, and more would air it throughout the day. So we planned ahead for staff to be available in shifts all Sunday afternoon to personally talk to those who called. Some asked how they could get copies of the program. Others shared their own halting stories of extreme tragedy and unhealed grief.

• • • • •

Our ability to pull off the *Journey Toward Forgiveness* documentary for national release opened the door to do more. We created almost one a year for about the next ten years with several teams of producers and videographers working. I think we all found the deeply researched work fascinating, timely, emotional, even personal. The titles included "Fierce Goodbye: Living in the Shadow of Suicide;" "Hunger No More: Faces behind the Facts;" "Shadow Voices:

Finding Hope in Mental Illness;" "Building on Faith: Making Poverty Housing History;" "Embracing Aging: Families Facing Change" (the video we were working on the day of the infamous impounded van ordeal); "Finding Hope in Recovery: One Day at a Time;" "Long Road Back: Ex-Offenders Struggle for Acceptance;" and "Waging Peace: Christian and Muslim Alternatives."

For me, this period was the pinnacle of my working years: truly life-changing work of national importance, offering hope and courage. When I was in the chicken house and scribbled my note about wanting to be a Christian writer of some sort, I never could have imagined national TV script writing for the Mennonite Church.

As we gained more experience and had need of more interviewers, we divided into teams of two or three to spread staff (and college interns) around to travel and videotape interviews all across the U.S. and some in Canada, with snippets being used in the documentaries. Each program also spawned a thorough and well-designed website for those wanting to learn more about the issues and persons on the programs. Sheri Hartzler was the perfect producer and organizer for countless production trips, and also did much interviewing herself, working with various website developers to create the sites that gave more background on the award-winning programs.

I especially remember meeting and interviewing a woman about my age for the documentary on mental illness. Lyn had lived a disturbingly chaotic life as she fought her illness as well as addictions to heroin, alcohol, and cigarettes. By the time I interviewed her for the documentary, she had kicked the first two, or as she said, was "clean."

"Heroin and alcohol were easy to conquer compared to my nemesis, nicotine," Lyn said in one of her most memorable lines. "It still *has* me."

Yet today she lives a relatively normal life and enjoys her nieces and nephews and other family members, even though she had no children of her own.

We keep in touch on Facebook and I am thrilled when I see her posts because that means she is doing ok. She does gorgeous photography. Several other folks I met or interviewed pop up now and then on Facebook as well and I take it to mean, all *is* well. I can't help but think by the very act of these persons sharing their stories on national TV and on the web, they were influenced and compelled to continue to stay healthy and fight their various illnesses.

Some outcomes that thrilled and moved us:

- After the *Shadow Voices* program was viewed by the Bucks County (Pennsylvania) Department of Mental Health and Disabilities, the deputy administrator there bought 60 copies of *Shadow Voices* for every police department in Bucks County. They planned to send board members to each police department to talk with them about how to respond to persons in a mental health crisis, and shared it with ministerial associations and school systems.
- The U.S Department of Health and Human Services highlighted *Shadow Voices* on their website for a while.
- The U.S. Substance Abuse and Mental Services administration awarded Mennonite Media a "Voice Award" for the *Shadow Voices* documentary. Burton was sent to Los Angeles to retrieve the award hosted by Mariel Hemingway. Yes, granddaughter of *that* Hemingway. Thousands of copies of the program were sold in English and dubbed in Spanish.

I will be forever grateful for the opportunity to dig so deeply into the topic of mental illness and absorb the stories they shared.

Closely related to that topic is of course the tragedy of suicide. We took on the subject for a program in 2005, after becoming aware of how often suicide is the result of untreated mental illness (or patients going off their medication). As we worked on that documentary none of us ever expected to be impacted so personally just two years later in 2007.

Because we were religious producers, we decided to delve into what happens when a Christian dies by suicide—and the theological differences between religious groups on this issue. So many families and survivors have been haunted for years by what happened to their loved one—not only what led to suicide—but did God have open arms for those so tormented in their lives on earth?

Many of us on staff found our own positions shifting as we shared the suffering of those who'd walked this dark valley, and pondered their stories of family members who'd died by suicide. We were grateful to folksinger Judy Collins for narrating the video and Kay Redfield Jamison, a clinical psychotherapist and bestselling author (who happens to have bipolar disorder), for sharing her personal journey of suicide attempts and recovery.

We as a staff were looking forward to the biennial Mennonite Convention, which was being held in San Jose, California (July 2007). Our suicide documentary was to be featured. Plus, in May, a fundraiser for Mennonite Media had been planned locally in Harrisonburg, featuring wonderful actors and comedians Lee Eshleman and Ted Swartz. Lee and Ted were friends of our whole staff. They had created a number of fun but deeply meaningful videos especially for youth that Mennonite Media taped, promoted, and sold, benefitting our bottom line immensely. The local event was scheduled to be their debut of a new play, *Live at Jacob's Ladder*, near the end of May. Well-known musician Ken Medema was scheduled to appear. It was going to be such an important and grand time for their work and their many local fans in the Shenandoah Valley.

My closest work colleague at the time, Sheri Hartzler, worked a side gig as the booking agent for Ted and Lee and was in their inner circle of friendship. She got the news first the day before the fundraiser: Lee had taken his own life. Stunned and heartbroken, she shared the news with the rest of us as delicately as possible. Obviously, as columnist Jim Bishop later wrote in *The Mennonite*, the show did *not* go on.

It was a watershed time for all of us: How could it happen? Some knew Lee struggled with bipolar illness, certainly, and his family and closest friends including Ted knew how severe it was at times. But the questions circled around and around in our saddened psyches. How could it be? Lee was a dedicated and dynamic Christian, sharing his faith through a medium—drama—that people were drawn to. And he was so so good; Ted & Lee together were like Abbott & Costello, or Lucy Ball & Desi Arnaz, maybe the Smothers Brothers. Pure magic and inspiration. How could…

The sentence will never be finished but our work on the documentary plumbing the many mysteries of suicide—and the loss of a dedicated Christian friend—helped us to understand this heartrending malady.

There is no doubt in my mind that we will meet Lee again someday in eternity. I think Christ himself would enjoy some of the hilarious acting and lines and stories Lee and his acting partner, Ted delivered, beautifully portraying Jesus and the questions the disciples had as they followed Him. Through Ted and Lee we became much more educated not only on Biblical stories and messages, but on the tragedy and reality of suicide in Christian homes and lives.

*Michelle Sawatzky, a member of the Canadian volleyball team for the 1996 Olympics, serving here as voice-over talent for radio spots titled "Parenting on the Edge," which later won a Gracie Award from American Women in Radio and Television.*

*Wayne Gehman, Jim Bowman (a longtime TV and freelancer videographer) and Melodie Davis pause after finishing video interviews in New York City on the issues of aging.*

Journey Toward Forgiveness *documentary filmed for airing on ABC-TV in 2001 led the way for Mennonite Media to produce ten documentaries for national airing at the discretion of local stations over the next dozen years.*

CHAPTER 14

# A Short Flight of *Shaping Families*

A Mennonite mother was on the phone, telling me the bare bones of her daughter being a victim of sexual abuse—at the hands of a Mennonite youth pastor. I asked her to pause then hurried to close my office door. I put my phone on speaker and began typing so I wouldn't miss any of her account.

Angela and Christopher (pseudonyms) were parents of four young adult daughters at the time. They said they had a close, happy family of well-adjusted, bright kids. But not too long after the youngest went away to college, she called home saying desperately, "Please help me." Their youth pastor, who had shown her much attention and "grooming" of the type that sexual predators frequently do over a period of years, finally stepped over the line during her senior year of high school. It was only as she got away from home that she felt empowered to tell her parents, even though they had wondered why she had become so distant and sad.

This topic felt very close to me: A good friend from school had also revealed her story at one point for our *Beyond the News: Sexual Abuse* video produced by Jerry Holsopple. So this mother on the phone, and her family were living their version of thousands (millions?) of heartbreaking stories. Here was a family and woman wanting to share their story with the motive of helping others, and stopping the terrible scourge. And in particular, seeing this perpetrator stopped.

Angela had heard about our radio program through church publications and was calling offering to share their story. Yes, they were available for interviews. Yes, their daughter was definitely supportive. My mind quickly speculated on perhaps interviewing this couple on a trip to visit my mother. Very doable. We set about making plans. Again, I was so thankful for the way our three-year media effort with the older medium of radio was touching lives.

My mind returned to another phone call, about seven years earlier, that indirectly helped these parents and daughter share their story on the new radio program we launched in 2011.

• • • • •

Earlier, back in 2005, a donor was on the phone wanting to speak to me. That arched my eyebrow right there, donors didn't usually end up talking to me. Unless I'd done something bad or stupid—spelled something wrong, made someone mad.

But she explained that her friend Peter Graber—whom donors *did* talk to, often—at the Mennonite Mission Network headquarters in Elkhart, Indiana, had suggested she call and talk to me about her questions.

"Why doesn't the Mennonite Church have an agency focusing on the needs of children, or even have them on their agenda? There is no 'office of children and family concerns'!" Betty Jeschke pointed this out with the concern of one who'd maybe asked that question of numerous others. My head went, well, *she's right.*

But why had Peter suggested she call me? Later I learned he recommended me because of my work writing the "Another Way" column—often on family issues, and various radio spot series focusing on family dilemmas. "Another Way" was appearing in *The Goshen News*—which also carried a column written by Betty's husband, Marlin Jeschke, a theologian and great scholar if there ever was one.

Betty and I chatted about the fact that there certainly was and are Mennonite curriculum materials for children, probably since the early 1900s. Also, many churches have girls' clubs or boys' clubs and certainly youth group and service opportunities are numerous throughout the church.

"But what I'm really interested in is scholars working to study and help families, perhaps through the various Mennonite colleges," Betty went on. She gave an example of a conference she helped pull together for scholars, practitioners (teachers and the like) on issues with children and media, and suggested there could be many ways to focus such a conference.

The year was 2005 and our director Burton, had been rumbling for a couple of years about starting an ongoing regular radio program focused on family issues or other topics—something that would be again an outreach for Mennonite churches on a united basis.

"I think that could be a revenue stream for us," Burton mused, at various times, recalling how eagerly fans had donated and raised money for the work of Family Life Network in Canada, which he headed earlier.

Betty's call (and not just the phone call) resonated with me, too, recalling the glory days of the *Heart to Heart* radio program, which I experienced early in my years at Mennonite Broadcasts. Betty was not speaking from a conservative "family values" perspective although she used that language sometimes, but thinking more of how many needs there were in our communities for family support: kids on drugs, abuse, effects of divorce on well-being, suicide, bullying, teen pregnancy. After she sent a sizeable gift for the general work of Mennonite Media, Burton put some of the concerns we were working on into a thank you letter. He emphasized how challenged overall our society is to demonstrate true love, acceptance, compassion, and justice.

• • • • •

The idea of a radio program continued to percolate over the next few years, but we were still very involved with TV documentary production (described in previous chapter)—and a lot of other projects.

Meanwhile, as I had time, I began to ponder how we could go about starting a new regular radio program. What would it take? Did we still have what it takes, or were we too busy with other efforts?

We always started new program ideas by brainstorming or writing out a Program Platform (and I liked to capitalize those letters at the top of a document). It was a practice left over from Ken's days as director, and a good way to develop and put meat on wild hare ideas. As with writing a book, once you officially are working on a statement of purpose, goals, and the bones of an outline, you're on the way! I did several rough drafts before even showing them to anyone else, and included some of Betty's comments on family and my own experiences over many years working on new products or programs.

I figured the next step would be to produce some pilot programs and test them with real radio station managers through visits. Or going to national conventions such as the National Religious Broadcasters (NRB), a trade association. If we wanted to be on religious radio stations, we needed to know the current trends, competition, and who was playing. We would likely aim for a mix of secular and religious stations with our new program—tricky ground to navigate.

In December 2006 through April 2007, I made a tour of about five radio stations including our own local WSVA radio station, which was instrumental in launching the long running *Mennonite Hour* program that began our organization. I also chalked in several stations in eastern Pennsylvania and northern Indiana. I took CDs with sample programs and prototypes, including one that was more of a "Sunday morning" type inspirational program, along with samples of an interview type program on family issues. In each location, I sat down with a manager or DJ for their candid feedback. The feedback seemed to be all positive, especially for a program on family issues.

We settled on a name for the new radio program, *Shaping Families*. The aforementioned NRB convention in 2009 was held in Nashville and Burton and I spent a couple days there to make some key contacts. I set up one-on-one breakfast meetings and played samples for several radio station owners who were top priority in Mennonite areas.

By this time, the writing was on the wall that there wouldn't be much more funding (non-church sources) for TV documentary production. Plus, a five-year-old agreement with Mennonite Mission Network was about to expire. As a budget squeeze for Mission Network (MMN), our funding would be decreased each year until they would no longer provide any funding for Mennonite Media. The thinking went that since we had several revenue streams such as producing and selling documentaries to viewers, and sales of older products, that we could carry on. But those trickles of income couldn't pay for all personnel.

It was a very difficult time for staff. When the human resources person from the MMN Elkhart office came to visit, I knew it was not a good sign. Still, I wasn't sure what was up. With finances down, cuts were surely coming.

When two of my longest cohorts both lost their jobs the same day, I so felt like walking out myself. If I'd been single, I might have, but with a two-income marriage partnership, that didn't feel fair to my spouse.

One co-worker had been there 45 years—even longer than retired director Ken. It truly was her life ever since graduating high school. She had worked hard, admirably, always championing the work of Mennonite Media, entering programs and broadcasts and videos into countless competitions, sending out mailings to radio stations, keeping files and files of records—records and data that were no longer so important to the new director, Burton. Lois was a splendid organizer, and for many years at the biennial Mennonite Conventions she directed the schedule and activities of the booth—

sometimes very large displays—and kept long, tiring days. My heart broke for Lois. She had been an enthusiastic supporter of the effort to get back into a regular radio program, and would have been so valuable working with stations.

A second cherished worker, Dorothy, was also let go at the same time. She had worked a combined total of 25 years as production coordinator and studio manager. Neither wanted any farewell parties; we as guilt-ridden survivors all understood, and said our goodbyes privately.

But our company still had—rent free—the resources of an awesome, fully-equipped recording studio, expertise and access to mailing lists for radio stations, and promotional channels through the church to see if a new radio program could fly. Lord knows there were enough issues to cover, people willing to tell their stories.

The show would move forward, a greatly tightened staff or no. We were down to 6.25 staff.

• • • • •

In January of 2010 we launched the first 15-minute program airing on about five stations. Gradually usage picked up—four months out we were on 12 stations.

Burton Buller served as host (on a volunteer basis as he was semi-retired) and I was the announcer—this time writing and voicing my own scripts (and flashing back to how I had written scripts for an announcer for the long-ago *Mennonite Hour* radio program). We went downstairs to the on-location studio (not to the old converted chicken house studio) every other week and recorded two programs at once, hooking earphones to our ears and mics to our shirts. Wayne Gehman, our video producer, painstakingly put the audio-only programs together on his computer. He was so helpful with scripts, too, helping me learn the wisdom of not getting ahead of myself writing a story, making sure things proceeded in orderly steps.

We also added stories from seven rotating voices from across the church, to the interview format. This helped provide variety and further pondering for listeners: Sam Heatwole sharing thoughts from "Frog Hollow," Natalie Francisco, Rebecca Thatcher Murcia, Harvey Yoder, Steve Carpenter, and Emily Ralph Servant, now a pastor. We paid them small stipends.

I had become a firm believer in the value for guests in such interview programs—and what the interview process does for them. Even when people have had disastrous, terrible things happen to them, somehow it seems to help to unload, open up, to tell their particular truth and story. At least after a time. In doing so, they often help others and themselves.

As Angela later told me in the recorded interviews on sexual abuse, "Your healing comes from telling someone. Your healing comes from therapy and talking about it. When people are silent—or when they tell a trusted adult and that person doesn't believe them, chances are they will never tell another person."

She cited statistics and added, "If they never talk about it, it comes out of their lives in other ways, usually in negative ways. So even if someone is an adult and was abused as a child, it is still therapeutic to tell someone, to talk about it, to get the evil out of you. But it is something that will always be with you."

Angela's words reminded me of another award ceremony I was fortunate to attend in New York City in 2009, shortly before we launched *Shaping Families*. Mennonite Media was the recipient of its second Gracie award, again from the American Women in Radio and Television. We had submitted our "Unsung: Family Voices on Mental Illness" radio spot campaign, sharing some of the wrenching stories of families dealing with this difficult illness. To me it was a strong signal that we at Mennonite Media had what it took for significant, national attention in radio.

Yes, there was a red carpet and I got to see luminaries such as Maya Angelou, Katie Couric, Jane Pauley, Rachael Ray and Mariska

Hargitay. But those who impressed me most were three women at my table. They had appeared in a documentary produced by the *Maryknoll (Catholic) Voices of Our World* radio program. It was called "Till fear do us part" and focused on domestic violence. The producer emphasized how the women were not "victims," but people who had become empowered by sharing their stories through the documentary.

I was somewhat blown away by listening to those who had experienced some of the worst things you can go through, and yet they were eager to encourage others going through difficult and soul-deadening times. They wanted others to hear how helpful reaching out to supportive communities can be. These women found they wanted to give back to others who are struggling.

After the award program, I emailed a thank you to other staff emphasizing the teamwork that it takes to produce an award-winning radio spot:

> It takes Burton saying, "Ah, but what is the listener to do with this information? What's your point of the spot?"
>
> It takes Dorothy going the extra mile with engineers in a couple of cities to clean up a noise on one spot that at first doesn't look like it can be cleaned up.
>
> It takes Lowell saying, "So how are those new spots coming along? We need to get this started in THIS budget year."
>
> It takes Sheri saying, "What have you done about this? Are you calling a meeting?"
>
> It takes Lois Hertzler pouring over mailing lists, making sure the right stations are getting the spots, making sure the right materials are prepared and proofread.

> It takes Wayne going back into old old projects and digital files, digging up needed interviews.
>
> It takes an off-staff designer, who puts her creativity to work in making an award-winning promotional package in its own right.
>
> It takes Lois Priest managing mailings and getting them shipped on time.
>
> It takes Kimberly, keeping the finances straight when producers hurriedly write down the wrong account numbers.

And finally, it takes persons with mental illness and their family members willing to share their stories before nationwide audiences, all in hopes of helping other people and reducing the stigma of mental illness.

• • • • •

Over the course of three years of the *Shaping Families* radio program, as the producer I had the privilege of interviewing people like singer Michael Card, pastor and bestselling author Brian McLaren, amazing singer/composer Ken Medema, church historian Martin Marty (visited his home and personal library), Mike Berenstain (of the Berenstain Bear book series), popular YouTube performer/comedian Josh Sundquist, and theologian Stanley Hauerwas. But perhaps even more meaningfull—everyday people opening up to tell their compelling stories of loss, hurt, rejection, divorce, dying from cancer, almost dying from a brain aneurism, losing a baby daughter just hours after she was born, getting beat up for being a different color, etc.

• • • • •

Meanwhile, throughout 2010 we (Mennonite Media, now using the temporary moniker of Third Way Media), continued conversations with Mennonite Publishing Network (MPN) in Scottdale, Pennsylvania. MPN had initiated looking into whether both companies would benefit from a merger. We were both facing hard financial realities, some of which came from the Mennonite denomination losing churches after its merger (2002), and overall, the shrinking of religious institutions in our society.

Over the years we had many meet ups with MPH/MPN staff. These happened either in our offices, theirs, or a reasonably-priced restaurant somewhere halfway between our two operations (roughly 200 miles apart). I always enjoyed opportunities to visit and interact with the staff at the publishing enterprise over the years because that had been my first choice for employment right out of college. It was the obvious place on any list of Mennonite communications or journalism majors at the time: a chance to work at "Scottdale." The town had almost become synonymous (at least for Mennonites) with the publishing operation there. At one point it hired hundreds of locals to run the printing presses and myriad jobs throughout the company.

We had sometimes reached across organizational lines to work on various media or curriculum projects. At one point we cooperated on a curriculum piece for adults using some of the *All God's People* videos that Ron Byler produced in the 90s, and created an expanded study guide, *Following God's Call.* An editor from Scottdale coached me on the ins and outs of curriculum writing. I loved working on it to give those videos further life and to introduce Mennonite small groups and Sunday school classes to the fine stories the videos conveyed. Jerry Holsopple also produced several groundbreaking rounds of video youth curricula. Later Sheri Hartzler and Wayne Gehman helped produce another cooperative video curriculum, *Via*, for beginning Christians.

Back in 2003, I was asked to attend a meeting of those creating a new children's curriculum for the Mennonite Church and Church of the Brethren, to replace the jointly sponsored *Gather 'Round* curriculum. I made a presentation on video products available or in production at Mennonite Media, reminding the committee that our world was moving into more and more religious applications of video. This was much to the chagrin of some present who felt that Sunday school was a sacred space from the digital world. I agreed I wished it was, but it was not reality.

But the encounter drew me into the heartbeat and mentality that seemed to exist for many in the church and the work of MPN at the time: Print ruled the day, and those of us at Mennonite Media felt our work pushed beyond print into newer media and beyond the church. The wish that children in Sunday school and other nurture settings could be in a sacred space, protected from the digital world—seems like, and was, a different generation. (Especially now from the perspective of what the COVID-19 pandemic of 2020-22 has wrought.)

After years of both competition and cooperation, the two organizations, both facing financial challenges, began talking and visualizing joining forces. Overall, the questions that conversations toward merger brought to the floor caused creeping concern and outright worry among staff in both locations. Who and what would be lost in such a merger? Some said it was more of a takeover.

Mennonite Media had begun of course as Mennonite Broadcasts, Inc., in the early 1950s and Mennonite Publishing House was started in 1898. Both had impressive ministries with various print and electronic programs for the general public, and books and congregational resources primarily for Mennonite churches.

Russ Eanes, director of MPN at the time and some board and staff were interested in combining the two operations and base it all in Harrisonburg. Some staff in Scottdale welcomed the idea of moving to a larger town like Harrisonburg—home to numerous colleges and a well-run Mennonite high school next door. I won't go into all the drama and logistics that I was not really part of as this was processed. But long-term, valued, and experienced employees, especially at Scottdale, faced the loss not only of their jobs, but the Scottdale community had their major employer close down. Staff of both organizations were on the firing line. Who would be let go? Who would be asked to move to Harrisonburg? Who would not be open to a move? Was it a takeover or a merger or a combination of the two?

The boards of both organizations eventually felt the time was right. The move to Harrisonburg took place over many months in 2011, and was officially launched at the Mennonite Convention in Pittsburgh, Pennsylvania, that summer. A committee working on a new name for the organization landed on "MennoMedia."

At first glance, the newish *Shaping Families* radio program looked like it would have been an obvious keeper for a publishing operation: An automatic place to immediately get on 15-25 radio stations with the latest author, the newest book. And surely, with programs on current issues such as drug abuse, sexual abuse and mental illness, our interviews were timely, well put together, and gripping.

We had endorsements from many listeners and station personnel, and this from Rosalynn Carter: "Compelling. I'm going to share it with the staff of my mental health program."

Listeners and station personnel wrote:

> We need more help in "shaping families." – Lorraine
>
> A breath of fresh air; talks about real life stuff – Caller to WBTX
>
> Appreciate everything you are trying to do and have done! – Crystal
>
> The speakers on *Sharing Families* touch on issues that really hit home with all of us. – Jim Snavely, program director
>
> I listened to your program last Saturday night and a lady was talking about how her husband had commit-

> ted suicide. I have had a lot of problems myself with depression and suicidal tendences so the program really caught my attention. – Listener, name withheld

There were undoubtedly thousands of listeners. Their occasional comments kept us going, focused, and hopeful. But there was no magic pot at the end of a rainbow, even though our development director Steve Carpenter kept the project in front of donors. A successful radio program works years to grab hold of and garner significant audiences—and solicit funds on air—which we didn't do.

Unfortunately, we had to close out the *Shaping Families* program in February of 2013, due to the agencies' tough economic times. In a farewell program, we told listeners that "After a generous start-up grant, we have grown to include over 20 radio stations and 10 sponsors. But we have not been able to secure funds to continue producing the program."

We were sad, but I knew there were new opportunities ahead.

• • • • •

In my heart I will always thank Betty Jeschke for her call that helped to launch even the short flight of *Shaping Families.* There were exciting days and months, although tedious in terms of grinding out a weekly 15-minute program. God knows our families need all the help they can get, or that we can give.

I say this partly because of the tragic death Betty's own son, James Miller, met. He was murdered in Goshen early Sunday morning in October of 2011 by a 25-year-old man. Betty herself died at age 88 in 2018 of multiple myeloma. After her first husband's death, Betty had provided an endowment for Religion and Science Conferences at Goshen College. Her second husband Marlin Jeschke, professor emeritus of philosophy and religion at Goshen, has written a religious column for *The Goshen News* for many years.

George B. Hinckley, President of the Church of Latter-Day Saints for some years has said, "Being humble means recognizing that we are not on earth to see how important we can become, but to see how much difference we can make in the lives of others." What a worthy goal. Working with the *Shaping Families* radio program—and before that our documentaries—reminded me of this quote. Betty, Burton, and our small staff helped nudge families in helpful directions. It ran for three good years. The program was basically a podcast, in the days before podcasts became so popular.

But there were other fish to fry.

*Burton Buller, director of Mennonite Media serving as program host and Melodie Davis as producer and announcer both enjoyed the interview style program,* Shaping Families, *which grew to air on 20 stations for its short duration.*

CHAPTER 15

# What I *Thought* I Always Wanted to Be

As I started thinking about when and how should I retire, I knew I didn't want to work so long that people would begin saying or asking themselves and each other, "I wonder when she'll retire?"

Was I getting stale? Over the hill? Should I make a late career move and try something else, like pick up some seminary studies? How do you figure out when it is time to move on? Burton had gracefully moved on as merger talks got serious, as he had many film and other projects he wished to pursue.

Back in 2013, Amy Gingerich as editorial director had tapped me as she shuffled responsibilities, and asked that I be one of three managing editors for the various product lines of MennoMedia. Valerie Weaver-Zercher would be the main editor especially acquiring new books and authors, with Mary Ann Weber picking up all curricula editing. I would work on special assignments such as republishing some older successful books with new formats and covers, and overseeing the relaunch of *Mennonite Community Cookbook* in 2015. Mary Ann, Valerie and I went to a three-day planning retreat and orientation near Amy's home in Cleveland. She was nearing the end of her second pregnancy and the doctor was not anxious for her to travel.

More change was afoot. To economize even more, there were rumblings that the building I had *lived* in for 42 years was going to be sold. It was definitely like home for me. I had been working there ever since graduation from college.

Russ Eanes, the new director for the combined company (see last chapter) had planned and survived one major sale of a longtime office and printing building (over 100 years) in Scottdale, Pennsylvania. In our Harrisonburg location, the nearby Mennonite high school made inquiries as to whether we were open to selling our MennoMedia building. We were next door to them and they had unofficially coveted our building, acreage, and precious road frontage for years. Or so the stories went.

It took a few years of negotiating a price. The school needed to figure out whether it had the support of donors to move ahead on such a major change, which would bring into one location all their K-12 students. MennoMedia also had homework to do—finding a warehouse that could handle hundreds of thousands of pieces of inventory (books, curricula, DVDs, hymnals). And, from my end, very, very sadly saying goodbye to more excellent and valued longtime employees as we moved steadily to downsize to smaller space. Those employees didn't deserve such an end.

That's why I never yearned to move further up the chain—I would have hated and likely not done well in streamlining operations. When others were "let go," I pondered quitting my own job. My close friend and colleague quit soon after the merger, in order to save the job of a colleague. For that she will get stars in heaven—and kudos for the challenging but rewarding mission endeavors she and her husband took up in Romania.

I didn't know what I would do if I quit, at my age, and without commuting to another city. With grandchildren now in the picture, my own coveting involved wanting to be available to spend more time with them as opportunities arose.

But I loved some of the challenges in front of me: researching and writing a 10-page history of the classic *Mennonite Community Cookbook* (author Mary Emma Showalter Eby) as well as serving as editor for a new cookbook by our popular Amish columnist, Lovina Eicher. Working with both the Showalter and Eicher families was a treat and challenge in many ways. Some Showalter family members were uncertain of adding photos to the legacy bestselling cookbook, one of the first major cookbooks ever published (1950) by Mennonites and Herald Press, and a solid royalty producer. The new edition required some careful negotiation with family members. I think most if not all the family were pleased with it in the end.

Lovina Eicher's family was anxious to produce a new cookbook under our publishing arm, but wisely hesitant about an editor, photographer, and food stylist descending on their private home for days on end. Earlier they had gone through days of cooking and living with non-Amish strangers in their midst for previous cookbooks. We determined to make that process as painless as possible, spreading out the cooking and photography over several months instead of all at one whack. I was privileged to spend one day in their home as Lovina and her daughters stirred, baked, and cooked for her cookbook—and I helped by trying to keep up with the stack of pans and dishes that needed washing.

Another Amish author I enjoyed working with (although I have not yet had the chance to meet her) was Canada-based Marianne Jantzi. A natural writer, we called her first book *Simple Pleasures: Stories from My Life as an Amish Mother.* She would talk to me from the phone shack out in their yard (a common practice among Amish to minimize the insert of technology inside their homes) about her progress and questions as she wrote. I felt a little like a grandma-at-a-distance in hearing her asides to her children—promising a popsicle if they were good while she talked to me on the phone.

• • • • •

At some point, Amy called me one day to discuss a decision she had made. I was spending approximately six to eight hours a week writing the newspaper column, "Another Way," and responding to readers. And it wasn't just my time on the column that concerned Amy, that she and likely our director, Russ, had discussed. It was the bookkeeper's time, a bit of time in shipping, and the customer service team who oversaw the billing process to newspapers—all of which happened with little involvement from me. "We feel like we could better use your time and writing skills by enhancing our editorial team's goals for publishing and marketing great Herald Press books." I don't remember her exact words but that was the gist.

I was not altogether surprised. Just a little sad that the day had come when I was being asked to drop the column. Truth be told, I had become over-busy with my new editorial assignments.

"Would you mind if I took it over on a personal level, outside of my work hours?" I asked slowly. It had been a great run for me—I loved writing the column and corresponding with thousands of readers over 30+ years and having a great space to share my column on the Third Way website. I tried in that space to frequently review key books published by Herald Press.

Amy said something like, "Oh absolutely, you can do as you like at home on your own time." I knew I would be writing anyway—the column sometimes served as a personal journal of sorts. And I would be paid a small fee by the newspapers if I could hang on to them. The newspaper industry was already dwindling, with less and less space in newspapers for personal and local columnists like me—those of us without a national following like Heloise or Abby.

This helped me feel a little of what my downsized colleagues had felt over the years: like what I did wasn't valued as much as I thought it was. It did hurt. Amy had shared the news in the kindest way possible, but life would go on.

• • • • •

I admired the job Amy was doing leading the whole editorial team including designers, editors, producers, and writers. She worked from her home in Ohio and I was accustomed to getting random and unannounced Skype calls in the middle of my work day. My theory was that she preferred visual contact over just voice, and she herself was always dressed for office work—not slouching in sweat pants and t-shirts.

By mid-2016, there was another Skype call.

"Melodie," she began with a serious smile on her face, "I've been wondering if you would like to try on a new role for us." I, as usual, was all ears for new challenges and opportunities, especially after all the changes we'd been through as a company.

"I'm thinking you would be good as our overall managing editor of all books passing through our system," she went on.

I was probably smiling, too, as thoughts of being named a real Herald Press editor after all these years went through my head. The job I thought I would be ready for right out of college (and of course was far too inexperienced for) was being dangled in front of my heart.

It probably didn't take me ten seconds to know I would say yes, but old hand that I was, I probably stalled with, "So what exactly does that involve?" Amy herself had worked that role at one time.

"Sometimes I call it the air traffic controller," grinned Amy. "We have our acquisitions editor bring a book into our house, and when she's finished editing and working with the author for a finished complete manuscript, you would send it to the copyeditor and receive it back, and then work with the author to incorporate or improve on the edits marked by the copyeditor."

"Oh yes, with Sara," I nodded. Sara worked off location also, from her home in Oregon.

"Then (or before then actually) you line up two proofreaders to do first and second rounds of proofreading," Amy paused again.

I pretty well knew the routine, and I was ready to jump. Would it be wrong to seem overeager? My heart was beating pretty fast, I was plain out excited for the new opportunity. A dream job! Not quite the top of the ladder but an integral part of the publishing team with a chance to work with dozens of authors—some newbies, some well-known at least in Mennonite circles.

"Sure!" I exclaimed, knowing that Amy already knew my answer.

Serving as managing editor of Herald Press books was stressful: lining up first and second proofreaders (most who worked as freelancers) months down the road to fit into their personal schedules and our book publication deadlines. And sometimes, I plain out messed up, overlooking that oh yes, I had our main proofreader, Ardell, scheduled to proof two major volumes at once. Somehow, he managed to always squeeze the deadlines forward, saving my hide another time.

Truly it was like an air traffic controller when you didn't want to allow anything big to smash up with another project. There was lining up big name authors or theologians (as well-known as possible) to write endorsements for books to put on the front or back cover. You went for the biggest name first and if she or he turned you down, you went down your list to middle list folks, all the while kind of implying that they were your first choice!

There was also fretting over what if a book comes out and you spell the author's name wrong—maybe not on the front of the book, but back there on the book's spine? Not a good thing to do and it never happened to me. But when it happened for one member of our staff, we were fortunate to have a very understanding author who did not fret or demand a reprint for one letter being off in spelling his name on a book spine. Overall in my 43 years of work, there were things we had to reprint because of a mistake or misspelling I made, and I was never asked to pay up for the error—just one of the hidden costs of the publishing industry. Or earlier, our media projects. People with forgiving bosses can be exceedingly thankful.

Amy Gingerich was named executive director for MennoMedia in late 2017 when Russ chose to "take a break" and do something different. This was the first female director I worked for, although two colleagues, Sheri Hartzler and Lowell Hertzler, had admirably shared the positions of co-directors in an interim period right before the 2011 merger.

When I think of my final boss at MennoMedia, Amy was much younger than all our other directors. She was of the generation so adept at adapting to new technology and using it well, lived out in her personal and public life. For instance, when we no longer could afford to have our own information technology staff person, she made herself point person for a new phone system in our new location, called Ring Central. She got us all on board with using it. I think she knew she could do it with little fanfare and at little expense, so wham-o, we were off and running. She also favored using Zoom for our meetings and asked us to learn how to set such up. This was in the days before great numbers started using Zoom because of Covid.

I was blessed to have good bosses or directors through 43 years of employment—which certainly helped with such a long tenure. Mostly men, but there were many fine women working anonymously behind the scenes. Some of our programming would never even have gotten off the ground, on the air, etc., without the gifts of these women and their tenaciousness.

• • • • •

The reality of working as the managing editor felt more like an assembly line than I expected. Keeping track of schedules. Pushing manuscripts back and forth through the careful proofing process. During this time I also served as editor of the long-running Herald Press magazine *Purpose* for about two years. I enjoyed that assignment, especially since it was one of the magazines that used some of my early writings. It was a fun outlet that was easy for me after serving as editor over 24 years (part time) for an independently run magazine, *Living for the Whole Family.*

Staff-wise, there was little budget for the frequent travels I had always looked forward to at Mennonite Media. Maybe the career I thought I wanted was not as exciting and adventurous as the work I had long enjoyed in my roles for Mennonite Media before the merger. It was an awakening to find that out.

Why did I stay so long? How could I stay inspired working for the same place all those years? As a local TV anchorman put it in retiring after 33 years for him in the same place, "Well, the *job* changed every couple years."

• • • • •

Going home from the last Mennonite Convention I would attend as a staff member (and I'll be forever grateful that our director, Amy, allowed me this blessing), my heart was full as I boarded the shuttle bus to the Orlando Airport. I had been privileged to attend something like sixteen Mennonite Conventions, missing some when I was pregnant or had a newborn. My hardworking blue-collar husband had been able to catch the flavor and excitement of at least three conventions as we arranged other travel to follow several of those extravaganzas.

On the bus I chanced to sit beside a long acquaintance from high school days, Cliff. (And excuse me while I play a bit of "Mennonite Game" here if you've heard that expression.) Cliff also happened to be the brother of the woman I first shadowed on the job at Mennonite Broadcasts, Linda Brubaker (whose efforts to train me are covered in Chapter 1 of this book). Cliff's mother had shared a table with my mother when they both were in rehab/nursing care at Greencroft Retirement Home (Indiana) a number of years ago. Mom was always so impressed that Cliff's father, Dean, had come every day to sit and watch his wife eat a meal, absolutely dedicated to her. Dr. Dean Brubaker was also our family dentist for many years.

Cliff and I discussed our aging parents, and how it felt to be aging ourselves. And then we were circling back to my very first meet-up with his sister, Linda, as she began to train me. How she had noted that there wouldn't be many people in the office that day, due to "everyone" being away at the Mennonite Convention in Eureka, Illinois. I had hoped to one day get to go to those conventions on company time. Done and done.

This larger circle was the Mennonite family that was undeniably part of my being a cradle Mennonite. As a child, this faith family had not yet widened into unfamiliar-sounding last names, different colors of skin and ethnicity, and wonderful new hymns in different languages and choruses but all ascending to the same God. Linda herself had passed 20 years earlier to that unbroken circle through cancer—far too early for the lovely family she left behind.

But on that ride to the airport, I felt a connection to the even wider circle of God's family that we had sought to reach through the multiple forms of communication that we embraced at Mennonite Media. Sometimes a little wobbly or fumbling, but always seeking to bring praise and insight to the God of our lives.

Even through the medium of song.

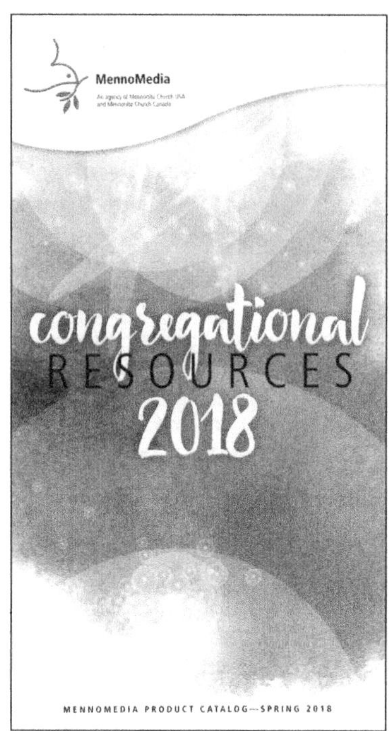

*Serving as a managing editor for Herald Press books and MennoMedia products should have been a dream come true. Like most jobs, it had its ups and downs.*

CHAPTER 16

# Ringside at One More Great Production

For the last six or so years of my tenure with MennoMedia I got a ringside seat in a completely new kind of media project for me: the making of a new hymnal. It was something I never expected to experience. But with the publishing arm's move from Scottdale, Pennsylvania, to Harrisonburg in 2011, this was the first Mennonite hymnal to be organized from Harrisonburg. Although, I will hasten to add, not the first Mennonite hymnal from the Shenandoah Valley, which is still in print—the *Harmonia Sacra*.

I was not on any of the hymnal work teams who labored so diligently for years, but was pulled in at various junctures for feedback, opinions, writing news releases, and assisting in raising funds to make it possible. In general, I was able to experience the enthusiasm and anticipation of the hymnal committee working on a holy new thing.

As early as 2013 or so, there were surveys sent out by our office asking congregants across the Mennonite churches what their favorite songs or hymns were—their "heart" songs. These were songs that moved them every time they sung them, or their favorites theologically—the words that expressed their deep faith understandings. These nominations would become the starting point for a future hymnal committee.

The lists of favorites sat, in hibernation I guess—or brewing until the time was right—for half a decade. Money had to be raised.

Musicians and theologians tapped to serve on the committee. Structures and additional staff hired to carry the workload. It was all new to me, and in a way I was glad not to be asked to jump into that overwhelming, detailed, and time-consuming staff work. Especially since I knew I wanted to retire sometime midway through the process.

I've lived through a number of other hymnal launches including in the denomination I now call home, the Presbyterian Church USA. A new Presbyterian hymnal launched in 2013, and they contracted as their interior designer a woman who also worked for the Mennonite Publishing House (Herald Press)—a fascinating factoid. I remember as a high school junior at Bethany Christian (Mennonite school) experiencing the first hymnal launch I ever knew in 1969, called simply *The Mennonite Hymnal.* Our choir learned some of the new songs to present to the student body and faculty at our school.

A year later (1970), when I entered the Mennonite Church's voluntary service program, in our two-week orientation experience, we were introduced to the incomparable "606" acapella anthem, "Praise God from Whom All Blessings Flow" in that hymnal. A music group also going through orientation called the *Cherchez-Vivre* (Search to Live), had the novel idea to do a year of voluntary service by singing and working across the U.S. and Canada. They mainly traveled to Mennonite communities or mission outposts. That song (and 606 number) was destined to become the heart song of many, many Mennonites.

It's an example, though, of how using an insider code can also quickly sort out, unfortunately, the "insiders" from the newcomers to the Mennonite Church. For instance, if you knew how to sing 606 acapella you were obviously in an inside group who knew how to harmonize while singing. If you couldn't quite join in, you were not "in." Thankfully, Mennonites are now working to change—along with the times—and are much more ethnically diverse than they once were.

Shortly before the hymnal launch of *Voices Together* in late 2020, I was intrigued—and happy—that one of the Mennonite schools (K-12) I'm aware of, has realized that if they want to live out their goals and values of truly being a school for people of all races and ethnic groups, they need to change their assumptions about the music they sing in their religious assemblies and chapel events. They could no longer assume they could just call out a hymnal number (even if they weren't using books) and expect everyone to know what the song was or how it went. Our personal or congregational music styles and preferences vary widely of course.

One of the most important aspects for this or any hymnal was doing major fundraising. The price you or a church pays out of pocket for any hymnal is fiercely underwritten by major donations and grants by organizations and individuals who believe in the importance of keeping congregational music alive.

This hymnal was fortunate to have the gifts, enthusiasm, and expertise of a longtime development director, Steve Carpenter. He was probably the first major fundraiser for a Mennonite hymnal project who first had a career in the Coast Guard, and later became a Mennonite through the ministry of Myron and Esther Augsburger at Washington (D.C.) Community Fellowship sometime in the 1980s.

I remember the first time Steve sat down in my office while he was working for nearby Virginia Mennonite Conference (an agency across the parking lot from our old Mennonite Media building). He was working on a bumper sticker at that time that would say "Blessed are the Peacemakers." He invited the collaboration of Mennonite Media saying something like, "There is a donor who is willing to pay the costs of creating the bumper sticker if you are willing to help promote, stock, and mail out the orders."

Steve was very convincing without twisting any arms. I'm sure he was that way as he courted and met with donors for *Voices Together*, too. There were bumps along the way of course between what a development and marketing fellow wanted to say, and what the hymnal committee felt comfortable with at times. But he and other staff worked carefully to entice people all across the churches (Mennonite Church USA and Mennonite Church Canada cooperated on this project) to get behind the new hymnal. Of course, there were those who questioned "How could it possibly be time for a new hymnal already?" and churches that had never had the budget or gotten around to purchasing the most recent *Hymnal: A Worship Book* (1992).

When Steve and the hymnal overall chairperson, Amy Gingerich, landed a major matching grant offered by the largely Mennonite-run agencies, Everence and Mennonite Central Committee, Steve's efforts on the fundraising end were resoundingly effective. The project rolled ahead, well-funded with new options to make gifts "in memory of" or "in honor of," which had never before been done. (And there are always those who don't gravitate towards too much emphasis being placed on recognition of donors.) These were things I enjoyed learning, being a little bit on the inside team.

The first major decision that we worked on as staff was how to go about naming that new collection. For many months (years even) it was simply called the "new Mennonite song collection." The hymnal committee also gave input but deciding on the title was not their task. They had enough to do sifting through (and prayerfully and thoughtfully singing through many songs) more than 10,000 pieces. They eventually narrowed the selections to just 775 (plus artwork and worship aids). That is still a pretty big number when compared to three earlier Mennonite hymnals: *Hymnal: A Worship Book* (1992), 658 songs; *The Mennonite Hymnal* (1969), 653 songs; *Church Hymnal* (1927), 657 songs. That was the one I grew up with.

All staff and committee members were invited to submit hymnal title possibilities and while I have no idea what I suggested, it was fun brainstorming real possibilities. As the list narrowed, the voting became more serious and, in the end, *Voices Together* worked very well for the goals of the project and stood out from previous hymnals and from those of other denominations. I loved (Is that petty?) being in the know about what titles were under consideration.

In the same way, as the designer got to work on cover treatments, I was excited to give feedback on Merrill Miller's efforts. Working with Herald Press designers through the years—Reuben Graham was our other book designer—was fun, hairpulling, exhilarating, exhausting, and ultimately heart-warming when we'd finally land on a design that most of the team could get behind. It was interesting to watch the various small tweaks and flourishes Merrill tried and tested on the hymnal cover—and to see the strong negative or positive responses from staff and others queried.

I don't think anyone had a harder job (unless the chair of the committee himself, Bradley Kauffman) than Karen Gonzol. She brought a background of working with details and recordkeeping until a task was figured out. There was plenty of figuring out to do on spreadsheets and clearances and permissions and obeying all the rules of such publications. Karen's shared office was next door to my space. She seemed to ride the ups and downs and frustrations of putting a hymnal together from scratch with deep commitment and excellent expertise.

• • • • •

Later, before the hymnal launch (and after my retirement in March of 2019), my connection to the project began to feel even more personal. My oldest daughter got an email from one of the editors at Herald Press, asking her to proof one of the indexes for the hymnal. As a mom, I squealed with delight that she was getting to work on this landmark book that would go down in history for the Mennonite churches.

When I was still on staff, Michelle was on my proofreading list of "occasional" proofers, partly because she already had a full-time job. Plus, she and her husband have three small sons. But she loved the gigs: the extra money, being able to work at all hours of the day or night, and she was a known grammar nerd among her friends and family.

As her mother, I tried not to either over-use or under-use her as a proofer. For the last 10 years or so she has been an active worship leader in a very small Mennonite congregation on the outskirts of Washington, D.C., where she put to use her excellent music and singing skills.

Michelle called saying, "The managing editor asked me a couple days ago if I could do some proofing on a short turnaround, and I always hate to say no because I want to keep being asked. But the deadline is Thursday!"

I groaned in sympathy.

Michelle went on: "After working five hours and only getting through eight out of thirty index pages, I told the editor, 'I don't think I'm going to finish by Thursday morning.'" The editor responded that Thursday *evening* would be ok.

"Um...I don't think I can make it by Thursday evening either," Michelle said with a sigh, and added she would try to finish it as quickly as she could.

Proofing an index is probably not anyone's favorite work, but it pays well—and it would be the index most heavily used by church worship planners like my daughter. So, she took a break from her usual work and got the job done just weeks away from the printing and launch of *Voices Together*. I also think of the team of women—including my boss's mother—who volunteered their time to tediously type out the verses of the various hymns and songs, because that is what the task required at one point in the process. There was no magical computer scan or pasting in of song texts.

Thus the historical book, which bore a little trace of my touch from the beginning days was now receiving a final check in one index by my eldest daughter—near the end of the process.

• • • • •

When most Christians talk about what they find most meaningful about worship, they say, "the music"—the congregational singing. I'm sure it is true for many different religions but I can only speak to Christian experiences.

This is especially true in Mennonite churches of many different varieties, cultures and nationalities. Music connects with the soul at a deep level, and frequently tears brim in the eyes of those singing or even just listening.

The music in *Voices Together* represents a wide variety of cultures, countries, and Christian theology—truly a book that many voices can enjoy, together worshipping the God who made us all. The hymnal has been a special, sacred, and holy media work, topping off my 43+ years with something like a halleluiah chorus.

We never know what lies ahead when walking with God through the paths God leads. Like the holy writ of the Bible, we can be assured that the work of compiling a hymnal will help thousands, perhaps millions in their worship of the Lord of their lives.

You never know when you start out, where your career path or life will take you. There will be surprises, disappointments, failures and, if you're watching closely, God leading you into new challenges and highpoints. Maybe you or your organization or business will become and do much more than you ever imagined, no matter what your field of work. God can and will work through us, just as God did through the amplification God provided for Moses through his brother Aaron (Exodus 4). God's work goes on in the world and we are invited to be a part of it in many ways.

To God be the glory. *Dios de la gloria.*

*Editorial, marketing, and hymnal staff (on Zoom screens from various locations across the country) share opinions and thoughts on the design for the cover of the newest Mennonite hymnal,* Voices Together, *released in late 2020. From top left to right: Valerie Weaver-Zercher, Melodie Davis, Amy Gingerich. Middle: Reuben Graham, Joe Questel, LeAnn Hamby. Bottom: Alyssa Bennett Smith, Bradley Kauffman, and Merrill Miller (designer).*

# Afterword

If anyone had had a crystal ball about an optimal time to release a hymnal, no one would have chosen 2020, and that presented a huge hurdle. The *Voices Together* team and staff managed as best they could to complete their tasks by Zoom and online resources.

As I am finishing up proofing this memoir in 2022—all the earth (at least North America) is coming awake and people are returning to in-church worship and connecting with friends. We have not stopped being the church in this pandemic time but oh how many missed the joy and deeply felt spiritual nudges commonly experienced while singing. I have faith the day will return when we may sing freely and heartily unto the Lord, unmasked, and maybe even hold hands or dance!

# Chronology of Programs and Organizational Names

**Chronology of organizational names:**

Crusaders of Christ - 1951

Mennonite Crusaders, Inc. - 1952

Mennonite Broadcasts, Inc. - 1956

MBM Media Ministries (within the church) - 1979 era

Media Ministries (with public) - 1979

Mennonite Media - 1989

Third Way Media - 2008

MennoMedia - 2011 to current time

**Chronology of major programs and projects:**

1949 *Heart to Heart* radio broadcast with Ruth Stoltzfus begun in McConnellsburg, Pennsylvania

1951 *Crusaders for Christ* first broadcast in Harrisonburg (same year I was born); renamed *The Mennonite Hour* in 1952

1951 B. Charles Hostetter named speaker for *The Mennonite Hour* (served until 1966)

1955 Home Bible Studies begun as follow-up for radio listeners

1956-1958 Navajo, Japanese, Italian and French broadcasts began

1958 *Heart to Heart* radio program transferred to Mennonite Broadcasts, Inc. Ella May Miller became speaker

1959-1960 German and Russian broadcasts began

1963 Kenneth J. Weaver named executive director of MBI

1966 David Augsburger named speaker for *The Mennonite Hour* (left 1975)

1967 First Inter Mennonite Media Consultation

1968 "Choice" radio spot series began

1969 First Mennonite TV spots released

1973 Lifeline Books became Choice Books

1977 *Your Time* replaced *Heart to Heart*, Margaret Foth named speaker

1978 *Art McPhee In Touch* daily radio program began

1979 Final *Mennonite Hour* program

1986 First *All God's People* video released

1987 "Another Way" newspaper column begun

1993 *Beyond the News* video series begun

1996 First *Cloud of Witnesses* video series released

1997 First *Rhythms of Peace* children's video released

1997 Choice Books sold over 2 million books

1998 Choice Books moved to a separate company

1998 *Third Way Café*, Internet ministry launched

1999 Burton Buller named second director of Mennonite Media

2001 First ABC-TV documentary released, *Journey Toward Forgiveness*

2004 *Fierce Goodbye: Living in the Shadow of Suicide* documentary released

2004 *Hunger No More: Faces Behind the Facts* documentary produced

2004 *Postcards from Nazareth*, fifteen 90-second radio spots and two 30-minute specials produced with tour guide in Nazareth Village

2005 *Shadow Voices: Finding Hope in Mental Illness* documentary launched December

2005 *Peace* DVD for youth produced

2006 *Building on Faith: Making Poverty Housing History* documentary aired

2006 DVD featuring the work and legacy of Mennonite musician Mary K. Oyer released

2007 Consultations with radio stations on new radio program options

2007 *Finding Hope in Recovery: One Day a Time* documentary released

2008 *Embracing Aging: Families Facing Change* documentary released

2008 *Unsung: Family Voices on Mental Illness* radio public service announcements released

2008 *Pax Service: Alternative to War* documentary premiered (produced by Burton Buller family)

2008 *Long Road Back: Ex-Offenders' Struggle for Acceptance* documentary released

2009 Name changed from Mennonite Media to Third Way Media

2009 Sheri Hartzler and Lowell Hertzler named co-directors of Third Way Media

2009 *Shaping Families* radio program launched (ended January 2012)

2009 *Who Are the Mennonites?* DVD launched

2009 *Via: Exploring the Way of Christ* new believers video curriculum launched with Mennonite Publishing Network

2011 Merger of Third Way Media with Mennonite Publishing Network/Herald Press, Russ Eanes named director

2011 New name MennoMedia announced

2012 Waging Peace: Muslim and Christian Alternatives

2017 Fall: four staff persons laid off; Russ Eanes leaves as director. Office moved to downtown Harrisonburg

2017 Amy Gingerich named director of MennoMedia

2021 Moved to Everence building in Park View, Harrisonburg

# Acknowledgments

Five women mentored me at the office, working behind the scenes. They and others like them were a strong component of any success we achieved over the years. Sheri Hartzler was a natural "organizer" and the one in almost every meeting who asked the "who is going to do this and by when" questions. She could also always, without fail, beat me at unpacking a suitcase when we shared a room on business travel, and neatly organizing toiletry items and make up in a hotel bathroom.

Early on, I appreciated the gifts of Evelyn Sauder. She was almost perpetually cheerful, loved typing, and could be cool even if she often got caught sweating other people's deadlines. Many times she knew an engineer was likely steaming at the controls in the studio, because a program writer or speaker was making last-minute edits, even when late getting to the studio. Evelyn, the typist, however, would always eek out their scripts—on a typewriter—just in time. Somehow. Using a typewriter (need I remind those under fifty)—especially under pressure and when mistakes were not acceptable—meant much higher stakes than using a keyboard where mistakes are often corrected right as you make them.

Then there was Lovina Troyer, who started out working for and grading Home Bible Studies. Her thoroughness got her promoted eventually to secretary, and then administrative assistant to the director. She had a gift for filing (and seeming to enjoy it), cheerfulness, offering support, enthusiasm, and fierce loyalty to whoever she was around.

I also pay tribute to Lois Hertzler who had the gift of managing schedules for projects, marketing expertise, proofreading, seeing to details, and exercising caution—a good thing in an operation such as ours. She started right out of high school and just kept going. She enjoyed the personal side of work—making friends rapidly.

A colleague I admired and worked with for many years was Dorothy Hartman. She was a stickler for detail and generous in working with graphic designers who hadn't quite caught the concept on their first drafts for various brochures, album covers, and video or DVD boxes. I loved her chutzpah to come back to work at Mennonite Media after having been let go in a budget squeeze. When she finally retired about a year and a few months after me, there were many roles she filled—almost anonymously—that needed to be covered.

I must also pay tribute to what I learned from my male mentors in media over the years as well. In interacting with male colleagues and bosses, I learned not to take things personally. Whether it was outright criticism, feedback, or editing something I'd written, it was not a personal attack. I observed how men could go after each other in a meeting—it was just putting your ideas on the table—and remain friends afterwards. Nothing personal. That is a great gift to learn.

I would love to mention many, many others, but personnel files were not opened to me and I surely would have forgotten numerous persons.

Finally, thanks to Michelle Sinclair, my daughter who provided punctual proofreading and copyediting, and J. Ron Byler for being so supportive at work and in his foreword.

Made in the USA
Monee, IL
27 August 2022